Dance
of the
Wolves

Dance
of the
Wolves

ROGER PETERS

McGraw-Hill Book Company
NEW YORK   ST. LOUIS   SAN FRANCISCO
TORONTO   HAMBURG   MEXICO

1 2 3 4 5 6 7 8 9 D O C D O C 8 7 6 5

ISBN 0-07-049580-7

LIBRARY OF CONGRESS CATALOGING IN PUBLICATION DATA

Peters, Roger.
Dance of the wolves.

1. Wolves. 2. Peters, Roger. 3. Zoologists—United
States—Biography. I. Title.
QL737.C22P46   1984   599.74'442   84-915
ISBN 0-07-049580-7

Book design by Nancy Dale Muldoon

TO BONNIE

Here is the distinct trail of a fox stretching a quarter of a mile across the pond. Now I am curious to know what had determined its graceful curvatures, its greater or less spaces and distinctness, and how surely they were consistent with the fluctuations of some mind, why they now lead me two steps to the right and then three to the left. . . . I know which way a mind wended this morning, what horizon it faced, by the setting of these tracks; whether it moved slowly or rapidly, by the greater or less intervals or distinctness, for the swiftest step leaves yet a lasting trace.

—HENRY DAVID THOREAU
January 30, 1841

Preface

This book is not a scientific treatise or treatment of the behavior of wolves. Rather it contains my subjective, impressionistic recollections of my experiences with wolves. Recollections are subject to the normal vicissitudes of memory, and in this book I have tried to weld anecdotal raw materials to tell an impressionistic tale and share with the general public the fascinating behavior of wolves.

Passages set off in italics are entirely fictional. Dialogues that appear in quotation marks are reconstructions from memory, not from notes. Even though the book is fictionalized, it does reflect my actual experiences with wolves and does faithfully describe the nature of wolf behavior in general and "Freya's" behavior in particular.

In order to preserve the privacy of individuals and the integrity of scientific research, names of actual persons, places and even wolves have been changed. Actions of different wolves and different persons at various times and locations have been combined and condensed to tell a tale. Any resemblances to real persons is inadvertent and unintentional. Any use of real names is accidental.

However, I must say that this book could not have been written were it not for the man here called "Dr. Hunt," whose enthusiasm inspires all who work with him and whose care, thoroughness, and integrity in the recording and interpretation of data are benchmarks for all field scientists.

I would like to express my admiration and affection for several others who made this book possible: Steve and Rachel Kaplan, whose brilliance and imagination inspired me to pursue lines of investigation far from mainstream cognitive psychology; Bonnie Clements, who may have gotten more than she bargained for; Bob Wageman, Don Whalen, and Steve Roderick, who I hope have not gotten less; Marilyn Jennings, whose humor, patience, and cache of pinon nuts made revisions more pleasant than I had any right to expect; and finally, the wolves Freya and Lotte, without whom there would have been no tale to tell.

Radioed Wolves

• Upsala Lake Pack
Freya, adult female
Frey, her mate
Loki and Odin, male pups

• Olympus Pack
Kronos, adult male
Hera, female pup
Zeus, male pup
three unradioed wolves

• Russian Lake Pack
Olga, adult female
Igor, adult male
Ivan, adult male
Yuri, male pup
five unradioed wolves

• Mogul Lake Pack
Behti, adult female
Akbar, adult male
two unradioed wolves

• Beach Lake Pack
Ann, adult female
unradioed mate

• Stabler Lake Pack
Bill, adult male
three unradioed wolves

• Lone Wolves and Transplants
Amy, adult female
Muff, adult female
1, 2, 3, and 4

Contents

1
The Naked Wolf

The wolfman strode smoothly, fifty pounds of camera equipment on his back, knees loose, hands in his pockets, whistling with a nice vibrato. For more than an hour I'd been bobbing along like a dinghy in his wake, taking three strides for every two of his. It was just light enough to tell that the overcast was solid.

We strode up a steep granite ridge and across a tiny waterfall and reached a small plateau where jack pine seedlings popped up green through ankle-deep soot soaked with rain: the edge of the burn. The wolfman removed his pack and sat on a ledge overlooking a long, gentle slope cleared by fire. I sat down beside him on the cold, wet granite. He put his lips to my ear and whispered that the rendezvous site was just below us.

Water dripped from the pines while a death watch beetle ticked off the minutes. I clenched my teeth to keep them from chattering and reminded myself that it was a privilege to be there in the woods, freezing in the rain with Dr. Thomas Hunt.

To students of wildlife, Hunt was a living legend. His dissertation, a study of wolves and bears in Wisconsin, had made his reputation before he'd received his degree. His book, *The Northland Wolf: Ecological Studies of a Wild Predator*, had been published in 1971. Now, only a year later, it was considered a definitive work on the wolf.

In an attempt to ignore the cold, I reviewed the events that had brought me to the wolfman's side. I was a graduate student in cognitive psychology at the University of Michigan. With Ray and Stephie Bach I was studying cognitive maps, the mental images that allow some people to avoid getting lost even in unmarked areas. This ability was of interest to the Forest Service, which provided funds that allowed us to let people explore several nearby forests and investigate the maps they drew.

Sam Halsey, the Forest Service official who monitored our grant, received our final report in person. He seemed particularly intrigued by my claim that the maps, and presumably the mental images they depicted, had four kinds of features: landmarks, routes, edges, and regions. It was Halsey who asked the innocuous question that was directly responsible for my current discomfort: "Why?"

My answer was Carveth Read's old idea that the Bachs and I called the "naked wolf" model: the hypothesis that many of our learning abilities are the legacy of the millions of years our ancestors spent living like wolves, cooperatively hunting for large animals over vast areas while their young waited at dens and rendezvous sites. This way of life would select strongly for the ability to remember routes and other geographic features.

Halsey took this conjecture more seriously than I expected. He explained that he administered a grant to Dr. Hunt, who, as it happened, was currently interviewing graduate students to work with him on a study of wolf territoriality. Would I be interested? Here was an ideal way to compare naked wolves to real ones, and it only took me a moment to recognize it. As soon as I did, I leapt at the chance to work with a scientist of Hunt's stature. Competition for the position would be tough, but I had not yet committed myself to a dissertation topic, and here was a rare chance to answer an interesting question in a way that was bound to be more fun than taking sophomores for hikes. I gave Halsey a résumé and asked him to have Hunt call me if he was interested.

Hunt called a week later to say he'd like to "look me over." I asked if the day after tomorrow would be soon enough. He said that would be fine and gave me directions to the Ontolagon Field Laboratory, near the town of Axe, a full day's drive to the north.

Two days later I left Ann Arbor, headed north. I drove all day, then pulled onto a dirt road and slept on the back seat. I woke up at dawn. The glass was coated with ice; it was August but I was almost in Canada. I rolled down a window to see where I was. I had parked on the shore of a large lake. Somewhere on the other side a moose was splashing water on its face. A line of pink appeared in the east; all around the lake, birds began to jabber. Filaments of steam rose off the lake, dissolving in the pearly light. I started the motor, watched the defroster punch holes in the rime, and drove into Axe for breakfast.

Axe is Edge City. In Ann Arbor it's a symbol of remoteness, a place for naughty children and banished bureaucrats: Siberia. It lies on a steep hill as though threatening to slide into the enormous open pit mine that once provided the town's existence. The last great forest wilderness on the continent begins at the city limits and is visible in four directions from the center of town. Nowadays the forest, not the mine, supports the local economy—through timber harvesting, tourism, and federal government—but some Axeites are miners still, commuting to the taconite stripmines that flourish along the Lake Superior shore.

There were six gas stations, one traffic light, and thirty-four bars, one for every 100 of Axe's advertised 3,400 souls. There were three restaurants, but only one was open at that hour. Its name was Stewart's, and it was a no-nonsense, coffee-in-mugs, workin'man's grill with reasonable prices, enormous helpings, and pieces of home-made pie displayed in a plastic cylinder. I had a piece while I waited for my ham, eggs, and hash browns; it was excellent. As I ate, I occupied myself with the road atlas I'd brought along as personal defense literature, an unnecessary move as no one paid me any attention. According to the atlas, one could head north from Axe and cross only one paved road en route to the North Pole.

After breakfast I used the phone ("No charge for local calls") to find out when Hunt would be getting in from checking his trapline. The directory was no thicker than a comic book and included not only Axe but three other municipalities of similar size. A large proportion of the Axe entries were the heading "U.S. Government"; one of these was "Wolf Project." That had to be it. I dialed the four-digit number and learned that Hunt would be in to meet me around noon.

With time to kill, I strolled through downtown Axe. The bars evidently did better than the restaurants, for several were open and already throbbing to the jukes. As I passed one called Pop's, I caught the poignant strains of the "Beer Barrel Polka."

On Taconite Street, a boulevard that brought new mean-

4

ing to the phrase "main drag," there was a theater that had evidently gone out of business. A tattered poster advertised Walt Disney's *Bambi*. In what I later learned was a typical gesture of backwoods innocence, the door was ajar. I strolled in. Amid the tawdry grandeur of Art Deco jukebox gothic was a glass-walled structure with its own entrance, labeled "Crying Gallery." I wondered whether it was for squalling infants or emotional adults. There was still a faint odor of buttered popcorn. I hoped the theater's closing was temporary. If things worked out, the Roxy would be my only source of cheap thrills for some time to come.

I stopped at Lep's Market for a toothbrush and a bumper sticker that said, "I am a Timber Savage from Jack Pine City," and headed for the woods.

I spent the next two hours happily strolling along moose and deer trails, finding to my surprise that even here there was little trackless wilderness. Everywhere an animal went, it made the way a little easier for the next—especially if the forerunner was a moose. Even the densest forest had been canalized into a network of paths, some well beaten and almost paved with deer droppings, others barely visible and suitable only for hares, but all providing structure for memory.

When I got to the lab, I was a few minutes early, so I explored, examining the rugged log construction of the lodge, cafeteria, bunkhouse, and office, that lay along a gravel drive. WPA, I guessed, noting how their solidity contrasted with the flimsiness of a couple of newer prefabs. Then I walked down to the Ontolagon River. The river slid viscously, a slick black mirror for the spruce and birch on the opposite shore. The pilings radiated perfect circles as I walked out onto the rickety dock. I won-

5

dered why the circles weren't distorted by the current. About a quarter of a mile upstream a small red car crossed the highway bridge, racing its reflection to a photo finish. A handful of goldeneyes glided downstream, moving Rorschachs in some inscrutable projective test. I heard a car coming up the drive and walked back to meet Dr. Hunt.

As he strode toward me the first things I noticed were his freshly pressed olive work shirt and matching trousers. Although I didn't know it at the time, Hunt's clothing had just given me my first lesson in Hunt's style, which is indifference to style. As I was soon to learn, what matters to him is not how things look but how they work.

I'm not sure what I expected a wolfman to look like, but certainly not apple-cheeked, moon-faced, balding, with an innocent openness in his smile. On the whole, I thought Hunt looked far more pastoral than predatory. It was only around his eyes that one could find a trace of wolf. At the foot of his high, tan forehead lurked two lean, dark eyebrows, incredulous predators ready to pounce. His eyes were almost hidden beneath them, gleaming in the darkness of their lairs.

Hunt invited me into a small cafeteria, where he began to unroll white paper charts onto the tables, holding the corners down with salt and pepper shakers. The charts showed only a few geographical features: the Lake Superior shore; some roads; Axe. These schematic maps were covered with red, green, and blue triangles, circles, and squares. "We trap wolves and put radio collars on them," he began. "We use number four and fourteen Newhouse-type leghold traps. Don't like 'em, but that's the only way to do it. The transmitters last a couple of years and have a range of about a mile on the ground and up to twenty miles from the air, which is how we usually track. We can observe their behavior, but so far my main interest has been in their movements and spatial organization, so usually I simply locate the pack, then fly on to the next one." He pointed to the charts. "Each symbol represents the location of a radioed wolf, usually with its pack." He looked up from the chart. His left eyebrow crouched. "What do you know about wolves?"

I gulped. I'd had only a few days for background reading. "*Canis lupus*, ancestors of the dog," I began. "They live in packs averaging six which allows them to kill animals their own size or larger. In the forties Young described a pack as a family-like group consisting of a mating pair and their offspring, and Schenkel claimed that they are territorial. They're listed as endangered, and population density is low even where they're not." I paused to draw a breath.

He raised a hand. "OK, wolves are territorial, I'd like to find out how these territories are maintained—what keeps wolves in their own territories or out of others', as the case may be. At the moment I've got eleven collars in five different packs and three collars on loners. I want to put out more. Trapping takes time, and so does homing in, so I need a couple of graduate students to help. I've got one already—Bert Cartwright from the University of California at Santa Barbara. He's going to work on howling. The other major mechanism in territory maintenance is probably scent marking, and that's the slot you could fill if you work out."

He paused and ran a hand over his scalp. "There's one more thing you should know," he said. "We're here to study wolves, not to save them. These are hard times for wolves, so detachment won't always be easy. The deer population in this area is dropping, and wolves depend

7

on deer for food. They may switch to beaver or moose, they may migrate out of the national forest, or they may starve. The deer decline is the result of ecological succession in old clear-cuts, hunting, poaching, road kills, wolf predation, and a series of hard winters. There's not much we can do about any of these factors, but in any case we're here as scientists, not as wildlife managers. If the wolves leave, we see where they go. If they starve, we see how long it takes."

I swallowed quickly, and nodded with deliberate nonchalance. Then I returned to the topic that had brought me to meet Hunt in the first place.

"Isn't it possible," I asked brightly, "that wolves learn to find their way around in their territory and that they avoid other territories because they couldn't hunt as efficiently there? Scent marks are certainly important, but they might well serve as landmarks, so I couldn't really deal with scent marking without dealing with spatial memory as well." I went on to explain some of the results I had obtained so far, but I left out the naked wolf. I wasn't ready to expose infant ideas to those carnivorous eyes.

Hunt agreed with my point about spatial memory but cautioned that any work we published together would have to stay close to the data. "Name of the game," I replied.

He glanced at his watch and said we'd better be off, because the plane was scheduled for one o'clock. Seldom slowing below sixty, he had us at the Forest Service seaplane base in twenty minutes. Hunt's nonstop commentary on the wolves we were going to locate soon had me muttering the names and ranges of Hunt's radioed wolves. The only breaks in his lecture occurred not in the many turns but when through some small opening in the whizz-

8

ing wall of trees he spotted a bird or deer—invisible to me—the doings of which he reported in detail. I throttled a sigh of relief as we reached the outskirts of Axe.

A few minutes later we pulled up to the dock. The plane was a Cessna 210 on floats. Its paint was chipped and faded, and there were dents on the fuselage. How, I wondered, do you dent an airplane? Hunt showed me how to install the radio-tracking antennas, one under each wing, and how to thread their cables through the cabin air intakes. Then I was introduced to the pilot, swarthy, black-haired Ralph Louis. Louis had been a torpedo bomber during World War II and now applied this exotic skill by slurry bombing, dropping loads of water on forest fires. He had logged more than 10,000 hours in the air and looked it. I clambered into the back seat, and Hunt and Louis sat up front.

The lake was glassy, so Louis made some waves, cruising across the lake at 40 knots, then cutting back across our wake to break the suction. The engine roared, and white needles danced across black dials. The whole instrument panel shook as we gathered speed. Suddenly we popped free. The plane, barely in the air, banked sharply to the left. We climbed and soon were bumping our way north at 3,500 feet, doing about 120. Hunt donned earphones and twiddled knobs on the receiver in his lap.

Numberless lakes glinted like tarnished silver as we caught their light, each going black as it slid below. Ridges rolled endlessly in an emerald surf; pink granite broke over every trough. Lake Superior lay like a rifle barrel on the horizon.

My enjoyment of the scenery ended abruptly when Hunt pointed slightly to the left of our course. The left wing snapped down, then returned as we leveled off on a new bearing. He pointed down; Louis cut the throttle and spun the trim wheel as we slowed to around ninety and began to sink. After about a minute of shallow descent Hunt said, "On the left." The left wing stabbed at the ground, and we slid sideways out of the sky. As we fell, Louis gave it full throttle and kicked in a lot of left rudder. We were suddenly whirling in a tight circle. "We're over a wolf," Hunt shouted above the engine's roar.

I reached for my binoculars and camera, but the acceleration pulled me down into my seat, and I could barely lift my arms. The ground looked as though someone had pulled a plug; the world was draining fast, and we were being sucked down with it. Hunt pointed past Louis's face and said, "There they are—three of 'em."

I stared into the whirling chaos but could see only spinning trees. "Where?" I shouted.

"Just below that tree," replied Louis, pointing down the wing.

I rolled my eyes—at that moment there were, conservatively, a million trees in view. "Which one?" I yelled back.

This time Hunt answered. "On the edge of the cliff, just above the swamp, there's a clearing with a boulder in it. They're in that clearing, on the side away from the swamp."

I looked intently, but every time I fixed on an object it threatened to go down the drain. Clammy sweat oozed from my forehead. I was losing my battle with airsickness. "Oh, yeah, there they are," I said, hoping to end the ordeal.

"Let's head for Beach Lake," said Hunt. We flew out of the circle and started a gradual climb. Then Louis lit the thick black cigar he'd been chewing. Holding my breath was only a temporary respite. Hunt turned to ask how I was feeling.

"Fine," I lied.

At Hunt's signal, Louis again cut the throttle. "Here we go again" I muttered as we went into another shallow glide. At the inevitable command the right wing dropped. I was on the right, and my window became the floor of a glass-bottomed boat. An army of spiky trees lanced up, a green phalanx charging. Then the power came on, and once again I was yanked down into my seat as we began our tightening gyre.

"This is Zeus, a pup in the Olympus pack," said Hunt.

I clenched my teeth and looked through the window-floor. By choosing a dead spruce as a landmark, I was able to maintain some degree of orientation and actually began to scan the area around the tree.

Hunt passed back the earphones. "The beeps will be loudest when the antenna is pointed right at him," he shouted. Sure enough, on every circle there was one point where the antenna pointed toward a tiny clearing. There were gray rocks and gray logs, but no gray wolves. I passed back the earphones, this time admitting that I hadn't seen the wolves. "Hard to get visuals in the summer," said Hunt consolingly. He tapped Louis on the shoulder and pointed west. Louis straightened us out and trimmed for a gentle climb. I opened a map of the Lawrence National Forest to the region ahead and kept track of our course with a finger.

Still climbing, we flew over Beach Lake, then over an enormous rectangular patch of bare brown earth, more than a mile on a side. Hordes of bilious green and yellow machines scuttled busily with invertebrate single-mindedness. Some had mouthparts specialized for grabbing or gouging; some, chelipeds for scraping; and others, carapaces cunningly adapted to hauling. Occasionally two would join in a brief trophallaxis, then return to their tasks. At one end of the wasteland were three square lakes the blue of antifreeze. To the north was the hive, where rows of identical rectangular cells lay precisely at the centers of rectangular lawns of an unnatural green.

"Gantry," Hunt shouted.

"Right," I replied, checking the name on my map. Sinclair Lewis would have loved it.

To my surprise, we began to circle the town. Hunt said something about lost data and pointed down the right wing. "In the back of the red pickup." There was only one red pickup in sight. In its bed a wolf lay on its side, legs stretched straight, a rope around its neck. I had seen my first real wild wolf. "Let's get out of here before the owner of that truck figures out what's going on," said Hunt.

I knew that the local wolves were listed as "endangered" under the Endangered Species Act of 1966. The carcass in the pickup bed was evidence of a federal offense. "Can you bust him for possession?" I asked.

"We can try," Hunt replied, then pointed north.

Ten bumpy minutes later we were circling a swamp near a gigantic burned-out area where blackened trees pointed up at us like accusing fingers. "This is the little Croix burn," announced Hunt. "Best one we've had around here." I wondered at the superlative, for I had not yet learned that forest ecologists regard natural fires with the same affection they feel for furry creatures—part of the Big Picture. A necessary part too, as I later learned, for jack pines seed only in fires, and berries flourish in their wakes.

Hunt pointed to a ridge between a swamp and a couple of beaver ponds. "We'll hike into there tomorrow. There's a rendezvous site on the edge of that swamp." On the way back to Axe he explained that rendezvous sites are places where adult wolves leave their pups toward the end of the summer, when the pups are old enough to be left for a while but are too small to keep up with their parents. Since pups are much less wary than adults, Hunt thought we might be able to observe and film them while their parents were away. He cautioned me that opportunities to observe wolves from the ground are extremely rare and that this enterprise was a thousand to one shot.

Axe appeared ahead, a toy train village without the trains. We came in steeply and splashed down about a mile from the seaplane base. Louis gave it three-quarters throttle but kept the flaps up, forcing the floats down into the water. As we neared the stable, untwirling dock, Hunt stepped out onto a float and warped us up. I crawled out to stand unsteadily on the float, the edge of the dock at eye level. I scrambled up and found myself betrayed— the dock seemed to sway like a pendulum.

The second stage of the Grand Prix d'Axe took us back to the lab, where we worked on radio collars, replacing dead batteries. Hunt tested their ranges by having me take them for a walk while he tuned them in. In order to simulate the electrical properties of a wolf's neck, I had to wear the collars on my biceps and thighs. They were awkward at first, but I soon forgot about them. I wondered if their intended wearers could ignore them as quickly.

When I got back to the lodge, Hunt was working on his field notes. He paused to explain that the first rule of fieldwork is "Write it down right away," then got back to work. I turned to my own notebook, in which I wearily scribbled my confused recollections of the fading day. I don't remember going to bed.

Well before dawn we clattered to Axe in a battered army jeep, a veteran of the Korean War. To my relief, not even

Hunt could get it over sixty. Unfortunately, however, the same rattling rods and banging shocks that prevented speed also precluded conversation. Two-lane blacktop reverted to one-lane mud top as we headed north on Mink Trail. We turned off onto an old railroad grade. The rails had been removed, but the ties had not. I pressed a hand against the metal roof to prevent my head from denting it. We bounced to the end of the road, stopped, stretched, and donned our packs. Hunt led the way. The minute we set out, it began to rain.

And that's how I came to sit on a cold rock in the rain, waiting for wolves that, I was sure, would never show up.

Suddenly there was a movement on the ridge to our right. I slowly turned my head. It was a wolf, long-legged and the same mixture of salmon and gray as the rocks around it. It looked our way, turned, and silently disappeared over the ridge. I tapped Hunt's shoulder and pointed. Slowly he began to unpack his cameras. Five minutes later the wolf was back, this time with another, identical in size and color. They walked slowly down the slope, angling slightly toward us. They seemed quite large, but suddenly a gray flash atop the ridge became another wolf, twice their size. It approached slowly, almost dragging its feet, then stopped abruptly and lowered its head to stare.

Its eyes were two gold moons in a stormy sky. There was nothing between us; this void was intimately immense, an interval of alien confrontation. As in the lengthening pause between far-off lightning and its thunder, each silent second spelled greater distance.

Then the wolf broke the bond. It shuffled a few steps to the left, circled like a dog about to sleep, and collapsed behind a log. I pantomimed with head on folded hands, raising my eyebrows in query. Hunt shrugged, then nod-

14

ded down the slope. The pups were playing on the boulders below, leaping from one to another in a crazy game of tag, chaser becoming chased without warning. Leggy but agile, they seemed oblivious of us as their game took them closer and closer. Then they, too, lowered their heads to stare and slowly approached, one to within ten yards. Hunt slowly raised his camera. When he pressed the button, his motorized Nikon shattered the silence. The closer pup bounced straight into the air on stiffened legs and came down running. The other stayed, though, and soon both were back, staring and sniffing. Shooting from the hip with my camera on my knee, I got off a few snicks as one of them once again lowered its head to stare. I blinked, and it trotted away. Soon the other pup faded into the forest, too.

An hour passed. The rain grew louder, rattling on the leaves and splashing on the rocks. Then the clouds brightened, and a few small patches of pale blue appeared. Hunt scribbled in a tiny spiral notebook. My camera was soaked; when I tried to rewind, the film wouldn't budge. My clothes were sodden, my back was stiff, and I could feel a cold brewing in my ears. None of this mattered, though, for hovering among the trees was an almost visible image of those pale gold eyes.

The sun came out. As soon as it got warm enough to make sitting bearable and walking onerous, Hunt stowed his cameras, stretched, and hoisted his pack. Once again I heeled. The walk back to the jeep did not seem long at all.

The rest of the day was a blur of dusty roads, whirling treetops, and wolf identification numbers. I fell asleep wondering whether I'd passed the test and dreamed I walked in an open wood where huge red asterisks lay like throw rugs on the forest floor.

2
Trapped

I woke deliciously disoriented; reconstructing my whereabouts was an amusing puzzle. The surrounding darkness held no clue. I sat up quickly and remembered where I was when my forehead collided inelastically with the bunk above, a kind of amnesia in reverse. Hunt was already up; it was the hollow thud of his footsteps on the basement stairs that had wakened me. I slid into my chilly jeans and stumbled to the kitchen for coffee.

Hunt did not drink coffee, however, and he had no patience for those who did. He reminded me that we'd be in the air for three hours and that there are no toilets in a Cessna. Furthermore, he pointed out, we had no time to spare—the plane was scheduled for six.

"No big deal," I said, struggling into my shirt and casting a longing glance at the cold percolator as I followed him out the door.

The jeep accelerated slowly enough to allow me to read the sign which explained the origin of the name "Ontolagon," a Dakotan word for the river and the area. It means "nowhere-in-between." It described my status perfectly; when would Hunt give some hint of how I was doing?

As we zoomed toward Axe, Hunt explained the procedure for radio tracking. "You fly to the wolf's last location, listening as you go. You tune the receiver to the frequency of the wolf you're after. A list of the frequencies is taped to the receiver lid. Twiddle the fine-tuning knob a little until you get your first beep; then tune for a clear, musical chirp. You'll have to keep the gain up at first—that's the sensitivity control, like the volume knob on a regular radio—but as soon as you get a signal, crank it down as far as you can. The lower the gain, the more precise your bearing will be and the longer the batteries will last. You always start your search at three or four thousand feet because the higher you are, the better the range of the receiver, but as soon as you get a signal, you want to take the plane down to get a tighter fix. Just point down, and the pilot will descend.

"You have a little switch that allows you to go from one antenna to the other. Keep switching back and forth, guiding the plane so the signal is the same on both antennas. That means you're heading either straight toward the wolf or straight away from it. You'll be able to tell right away if you're a hundred eighty degrees off, because the signal will get weaker instead of stronger. If that happens, just tell the pilot to do a one-eighty.

"Keep working the gain down, and when you go over the wolf, the signals will come in a lot louder. Switch antennas immediately, decide which one gives the stronger signal, and circle on that side. As you circle, switch to the outside antenna from time to time. If the signal is always stronger on the inside antenna, the wolf is in your circle. If not, move your circle in the direction of the

17

loudest beeps. After a while you'll develop the ability to tell exactly where the beeps are coming from. You'll sight down the antenna and see the wolf. There are forms to fill out for every wolf you find. Be sure of the location, legal description as well as verbal. If you don't know where you are ask the pilot. The pilots know every lake and swamp. Got it?"

"What's a legal description?" I asked, wondering if he'd be telling me all this stuff if I wasn't a contender for a position on the wolf project.

"A legal description locates places in terms of the townships and ranges, which are the coordinates on the margins of the Forest map; and sections, which are the one-mile squares on the map itself. Legal descriptions are important because place names are ambiguous—there are three Blueberry Lakes within twenty miles of here." I nodded and tried to jot some of it down as we slued around the last turn before Axe.

As we pulled up to the dock, Ralph Louis was attaching the second antenna, the stump of a cigar clenched in his teeth. My stomach churned in unhappy anticipation as I climbed into the back seat. We taxied out onto the lake, and Hunt handed me the receiver, clipboard with forms and map, headphones, and antenna switch. By the time I got them sorted out we were in the air. "We'll start with Zeus," Hunt shouted. "Let's head for Olympus Mountain."

I put on the earphones, clicked on the receiver, and was instantly deafened by a hissing roar. I turned the gain all the way down, then gingerly worked it back up. I tuned to Zeus's frequency and began to twiddle the fine-tuning knob. There was nothing on the headphones but a hiss. More twiddling, more hiss. We circled lazily. I heard no beeps.

I pointed up for more altitude and continued to twiddle. When we got to 5,000 feet, I thought I heard a beep. I stopped twiddling and turned up the gain as high as I could bear. I had just about decided that the beep had been either a hallucination or the squeak of the hinges on the receiver lid when I thought I heard another. By that time, though, I could hear beeps whenever I wanted. Then came a beep that was definitely a beep, on the right antenna.

I reached forward and pointed right. Then I got a beep on the left. I pointed left and got a series of beeps from both antennas.

They grew weaker, so I shouted, "One-eighty." Louis swung us smartly around. The signal was still there, so I pointed down. He cut the throttle, and the plane lurched as though it had hit a wall, then nosed down. As we continued our descent, the beeps grew louder on the left, so I pointed that way. They evened out. I had the gain only halfway down when the beeps began to fade. I signaled for another 180, trying not to imagine what Hunt was thinking. I got the gain way down, and this time the signals suddenly increased in volume, as he'd said they would.

They seemed louder on the left antenna, so I shouted, "Left." Louis punched the throttle and stood the plane on its left wing. The receiver suddenly weighed about thirty pounds. The beeps were clear even with the gain all the way down, and there were, thank God, no signals on the outside antenna, now pointing at the sky. Zeus was somewhere in our circle.

The forest whirled below us. Hundreds of wolves could be down there, rearing on their hind legs and waving, and we'd never see them. Hunt told Louis to take us up.

After the aerobatics I'd put us through, I had no idea

where we were, but Hunt knew the forest better than his own backyard. He pointed out our location, then explained how to record it on the flight sheet in terms of township, range, and section. I filled out the form as quickly as I could, for even though the ground below now rotated at a lazy 33⅓ rpm, every time I took my eyes off it my brain began to spin in the opposite direction.

I homed in on the rest of the Olympus pack with only a little less difficulty, and again the wolves were invisible in the trees. By the time I recorded their putative location, I didn't care whether I ever saw a wolf from the air or not. At Hunt's request I gratefully passed the headphones, antenna switch, and the clipboard forward and sat back.

With Hunt in control, we made a beeline to the next pack. Soon we were in a shallow descent, straight as an arrow, flying over a vast clear-cut wasteland studded with slash piles and rocks. Hunt handed me the earphones, which produced bell-like chirps—exactly the same on each antenna. He held the receiver so I could see it and slowly reduced the gain. The chirps stayed loud and clear. Three deer ran over the brow of the hill, and the chirps became tiny shrieks. "Something spooked them," shouted Hunt. "There they are, at the edge of the clear-cut, ahead and to the right." As we zoomed over the top of the hill, I got a tachistoscopic glimpse of a wolf standing in the open, tongue lolling, staring after the deer as they bounced into the woods a quarter of a mile away, tails flagging.

My zigzagging had burned up a lot of fuel, so Hunt found the next three packs. We made three long, straight approaches with a single circle at the end of each, then a quick climb to orient and get the next signal. It was a *tour de force* that I fully appreciated only years later, after scores of unsuccessful attempts to duplicate Hunt's feat.

At last our floats splashed onto Ishpena Lake, and we taxied to the dock. I wondered whether a brief glimpse of an exhausted wolf standing on a clear-cut ridge was worth it.

Hunt slung the Dodge around the last bend in the dirt drive to the lab, narrowly avoiding the remains of a once-blue VW squareback parked in front of the garage. It wouldn't have mattered if he had hit it. The VW had been rolled at least twice—once sufficiently long ago for the scratches and dents to rust and once so recently that the new abrasions were still shiny. Its windows were collages of cardboard and duct tape. One coat hanger secured the hood, another had been jammed into the antenna socket, and a third held a crumpled license plate to a bracket that once held a rear bumper.

Characteristically, Hunt ignored the car's appearance, merely surmising that it must belong to Cartwright, the graduate student who was to study howling. We went off in search of him.

He was nowhere in sight, but on the porch were a radio-tracking receiver and a portable tape recorder, both running. A poor human imitation of a howl wailed from the receiver. The receiver howled again, then swore, mildly and tinnily. A moment later a long-haired, khaki-clad figure wearing a nervous grin and a radio collar strode from the woods.

"You must be Bert Cartwright," Hunt said, extending his hand.

The grin flashed again. "Did you hear anything?" he asked.

"Yeah, I think your receiver is oscillating. Either that or there's a grasshopper mouse inside," I replied.

"Then you heard the howls?"

"And the swearing," Hunt added. As Bert rewound his tape, I asked to see the collar. He slid it over his head and handed it to me. It had a small throat mike built into the inner surface.

"What kind of range do you get?" asked Hunt.

"That's what I'm working on right now. So far it looks as if you could hear the howl farther away than you could get the signal. But if I boost the power, battery life goes down. I'll figure something out."

Hunt asked if he was concerned about moisture getting into the transmitter through the microphone. His own success in radio location of wild animals was due largely to his technique for producing a hermetic seal of dental acrylic around the transmitter. Bert replied that that was another bug he had to work out. Hunt left for the basement, explaining that he had to repair a radio collar.

Bert and I cautiously compared our impressions of Hunt. Both of us had been puzzled by an odd paragraph in the epilogue to his book, in which he apologizes to a wolf named Hurricane that he raised in his home. We found the apology inconsistent with the dispassionate, analytical Hunt we had met. Bert pointed out that in a later chapter Hunt describes Hurricane's escape from his backyard and her subsequent misery on a tether in terms that are anything but dispassionate and analytical.

"He doesn't have her now, though," I replied. "I wonder what became of her?"

Our conversation ended abruptly as Hunt stomped up from the basement, reeking of acrylic from the radio collars he'd been assembling. He offered to cook if we'd clean up. After dinner he announced that we'd leave at 5:00 A.M. to set and check traps.

* * *

Icy air streamed into the jeep through a dozen tiny crevices, somehow failing to dilute the stench of wolf bait billowing invisibly from the Mason jar between my feet. My fourth morning in the north was as cold as the preceding ones. If this was August, what would February be like? I wondered if I'd have a chance to find out. I cursed the fate that had made me the only member of the party small enough to fit in the rear of the jeep. The recipe for the wolf bait was classified, but as its odors overran one piece of nasal tissue after another, I could detect vinegar, rancid butter, asafetida, and decaying shellfish.

Hunt maintained a nonstop monologue of trapper's lore. He explained that he'd learned the fine points of wolf trapping from Thomas Mains, a professional wolf trapper who sometimes worked on the wolf project when Hunt was tied up with office duties. It was Mains who had provided the wolf bait and urine, the latter collected from the sloping floors of cages in which he kept several captive wolves. Hunt and Mains each averaged about 200 trap nights per wolf capture; that meant 20 traps out for ten nights, 50 traps out for four nights, and so on. Since setting a trap properly takes anywhere from half an hour to an hour, he continued, and since the traps have to be checked every morning, the investment of time is enormous. Traps are set on or near roads, so all of them can be checked in a morning. To prevent passersby from harming the wolf and to prevent the wolf from harming itself by pulling against solid resistance, each trap has a drag that allows the animal to move off a short distance until the drag, an anchor-shaped hook, becomes tangled in brush. The wolf may pull the drag free, but it soon becomes tangled again, gradually tiring the wolf and leaving a fairly distinct trail. Eventually the drag immobilizes the wolf, but it provides enough give so that if the wolf does yank, it won't do itself serious harm.

Hunt slowed to inspect the first trap, which he had set the previous morning. He pointed to an area just off the shoulder, indistinguishable from its surroundings. Because wolves, he said, have an uncanny ability to detect the slightest disturbance of the ground, much of the art of wolf trapping lies in reproducing the exact texture of the site.

In the next half hour we passed half a dozen other traps, equally invisible. Hunt paused at the last of these to point out a set of wolf tracks in the dust at the edge of the road. They headed straight toward the trap but at the last moment swerved out onto the road, then back onto the original course. Somehow the wolf had avoided the trap, probably smelling it.

A few hundred yards past this trap Hunt stopped in the middle of the road. Asking us to remain in the jeep, he donned a pair of gloves and removed a trap from a box attached to the rear of the jeep. It was like a cartoonist's version of a bear trap, but there was nothing amusing about it. The bent steel springs were two fingers wide, and the jaws were longer than my hand. Even uncocked, it had the utilitarian ugliness of a snub-nosed .38.

Hunt placed one end of plastic hall runner across his knee and cocked the trap as though he were breaking a stick. He made it look easy, so I asked him about the springs. He explained that the traps were weakened either by use or by removal of one spring. I supposed that if the trap were too weak to hold the leg firmly, the wolf could seriously abrade its leg by moving it between the jaws. I glanced at Bert to see how he reacted to the sight of the trap. He was intently scrutinizing a sparrow perched on a branch ten yards away. As far as I could tell, the sparrow was just sitting there.

After gingerly placing the cocked trap on the ground, Hunt unrolled the plastic runner perpendicular to the road, walked out to its end, and dug a shallow pit for the trap. With the trap nestled in the pit, he walked about thirty yards down the road until he found an area with exactly the same combination of soil and vegetation as the trap site. He scraped the top layer into a small bucket and returned to sift the soil over the trap with a flat screen-bottomed box. A few drops of wolf bait were applied to the side of a stump just behind the trap. I could smell the liquid from the jeep, ten yards away.

Stepping back, Hunt cocked his head to appraise his work. A muttered "huh," and he was down the road again, searching the shoulder. A few minutes later he was back with a handful of weeds and yellow birch leaves. He sprinkled the leaves, by extending his hand above his head and letting them float down, then shook the weeds in the same way. I couldn't see anything happen, but I guessed that he was shaking seeds from the ends of the stalks. He stepped back once more. "That'll do," he muttered as he strode down the road for the third time. He returned with a broom of weeds and whisked the ground as he backed up, rerolling the runner.

With the gear back in the box at the rear of the jeep, we rattled down the road to the next trap site. Hunt did five more sets that morning. No two were exactly alike, but there was always the same meticulous care to prevent contamination by human odor and the same consummate craftsmanship in reconstructing the surface. Another of the traps was baited with wolf bait and two were with wolf urine. Two others were blind sets, with no bait at all. These were placed on regularly used trails, between rocks or other natural obstacles that would encourage the wolf to step into the trap.

Every mile or so we slowed to check traps on the side of the road. Two were undisturbed, but the third was missing. Hunt and Bert were out of the jeep in an instant.

"Got a wolf?" I asked as I climbed over the seat.

"Don't slam the door," Hunt answered. A moment later he added, "I don't think it's a wolf—the ground isn't torn up much. It's probably a fox." He was right. A bright orange fox lay under a bush just off the road. Only its eyes moved, darting from one of us to another as we approached. The jaws of the trap had clamped its right foreleg just above the elbow.

Bert came up behind us and snapped some pictures. Hunt crouched before the fox and edged slowly forward. His arm snaked out, and in an instant he was holding the fox by the scruff of its neck, the trap dangling. "Get the trap off him," he said calmly. I grabbed the springs and squeezed with both hands, but they wouldn't budge. Hunt carried the fox over to a large rock and placed the trap over it. I leaned onto the springs with the heels of my hands. They compressed about a quarter of an inch. I tried to put the trap over my knee, but the fox's leg flexed sickeningly where the jaws held it. Hunt asked for a knife. Bert passed him the one he wore on his belt. Hunt tested its edge on his thumb, winced, made a short, quick slash, and the trap was off, still holding the fox's paw and half its foreleg.

There was no reaction from the fox. I supposed the pain of amputation was minor compared to that of the trap. Hunt inspected the stump, felt for further injuries, and, finding none, placed the fox on the ground. He released its neck and stepped back quickly. The fox froze, looked around, then shot off, running faster on three legs than I thought it could on four.

"No point in resetting this trap with all this human sign around here," said Hunt. "Put it in the jeep, will you?" I grabbed the trap by the chain, trying not to look at its grisly catch as I made myself an accessory to the crime. Bert was at the jeep, rewinding film. I avoided his eyes as I slung the trap through the tailgate. Bert looked a little pale as he took his seat, but Hunt actually whistled as we started down the road.

Several times we slowed to check traps, which to my relief remained unsprung. A mile or so east of where we'd caught the fox, another trap had been sprung. It lay in its little pit with no sign that anything had been caught. Hunt climbed out and examined the ground around the trap. "This one was baited with meat scraps," he explained. "Probably a weasel set off the trap, and it missed him. Weasels don't leave much sign in this kind of soil."

The next trap had been pulled twenty yards before its drag had hung up in a pile of rocks. It held a long dark creature that looked like a huge mink. "A fisher," Hunt announced. I confessed that I had never heard of it. Hunt explained that fishers are rare and are seldom seen. They are members of the weasel family, Mustelidae, they eat hares and porcupines, and they are found only in northern forests. He hoped to someday have the time to put radios on some and find out about their ranges and social organization.

Hunt checked the drag to make sure it was firmly caught, then cut a forked stick with Bert's knife, which he handed over without being asked. He pinned the fisher's neck to the ground with the fork and asked me to hold the stick.

I grasped it firmly, but the fisher didn't move a muscle. Hunt grunted as he opened the trap by kneeling on the springs. The fisher was caught by the toes of a forefoot. Hunt felt the paw, and then stood up. "He's OK," he said. "You can let him go." I pulled the stick away. The fisher did not move. "Let's get out of here," he suggested. "This guy has had enough stress." Bert's Nikon clacked once more, and we were off. I glanced back when we reached the road. The fisher still hadn't moved.

We whined down the dusty road a mile or so, then turned off onto a dirt road that climbed steeply to the south. According to the map in my lap, we were headed for October Lake. Voicing my concerns more directly than I ever could myself, Bert asked Hunt if there was some way to avoid catching smaller animals. Hunt shook his head. We bounced along for a moment before he added, "I wish there were."

For the next five minutes the only sounds came from the jeep. Suddenly Hunt pulled over to where an old logging road came in from the east. At the junction a shallow hole showed where a trap had been. Hunt was out of the jeep instantly and hunkered down to inspect the soft dust at the edge of the road. A set of doglike tracks led to the hole, then veered left to climb the bank, accompanied by shallow gouges left by the drag.

"Cut a straight pole about six feet long," Hunt whispered. Bert strode to the side of the road, grabbed a sapling, bent it, and slashed at the bend. The knife sliced cleanly through, and Bert hurried back, stripping branches. Hunt was stuffing his pockets with small vials, disposable syringes, and spare needles. He passed Bert a radio collar, grabbed a rope and a small spring scale, and started up the logging road, watching the marks left by the drag.

28

"We'll go up this road a bit, then make a circle, looking for his trail," he whispered without slowing. Technically his gait was a walk, but we could keep up only with effort. Bert soon dropped behind Hunt and I pumped along at the rear. I shifted into a jog, which required keeping my eyes on my footing, so I nearly collided with Bert when Hunt froze in midstride, extended his open hand, palm down, and gave the air two sharp pats. Ahead and to the right I could hear something crashing in an alder thicket, then a muffled clank as the drag hit a rock. Hunt reached back, and I passed him the stick. We stole slowly forward, one step at a time. Hunt pointed into the alders, but I couldn't see anything except leaves.

I took one small step forward and suddenly was looking into a pale golden eye. It moved, and there were two eyes, then white teeth, snapping at the alders. The wolf's coat was perfect camouflage as it crouched among the shadows. The wolf was not hiding, however. It bit through alder saplings the size of broomsticks one after another, nipping each one cleanly, as though it were a carrot. It growled softly between bites.

Hunt fitted a needle to a syringe, jabbed a vial, and held it upside down to draw some of the drug. He tapped the syringe, read the scale, squirted some liquid, and repeated the procedure with a second vial. "The first drug is Sernylan, a tranquilizer. The second is Sparine, a muscle relaxant that alleviates the convulsions sometimes caused by the Sernylan. Stay back here. I'm going to stick him." He attached the syringe to the pole, then sidled through the alders, weaving the pole ahead of him.

The wolf sprang to its feet, growling softly, and backed away, its lips curled in a primeval warning. The chain came taut, preventing further retreat. Never taking his eyes off the wolf, Hunt circled around toward the wolf's rear. I wondered what I should do if the wolf went for Hunt. I spotted a softball-sized rock and, feeling extremely foolish, picked it up, hoping that Bert and Hunt wouldn't notice. Hunt was now behind the wolf, which tried to whirl to face him but was unable to do so because of the trap, now clearly visible on its right forepaw. At the other end of the chain the drag didn't seem to be caught all that firmly. I surreptitiously dropped my rock and got ready to dive for the drag.

Hunt moved in. The wolf crouched, still snarling, then backed away, but the chain looped around a sapling, once again preventing retreat. The trapped foreleg was now stretched straight out as the wolf strained to get away from Hunt. Lowering the syringe, he moved slightly to the side, then lunged, jabbing the syringe at the wolf's hindquarters. When he pulled back, the syringe remained, the needle stuck into the wolf's left hip. The wolf grabbed it with its teeth, yanked it out and flung it into the brush. Hunt backed away.

He joined us a few seconds later, beckoned, and walked out to the logging road. When we joined him, he explained that it would take about half an hour for the drug to take effect. Bert and I sat on a fallen tree to wait.

Hunt began setting up his radio collar paraphernalia: a Yankee screwdriver drill, test tubes with rubber stoppers, sheet metal screws, ear tags, pliers, a red bandanna, and the collar itself, a fat crescent of pink plastic with a wide strap. I asked if the collars bothered the wolves. Hunt replied that the wolves seemed to get used to them and that they were probably no more uncomfortable than dog collars. "When you watch a pack from the air, it's often hard to tell which one is wearing the collar," he said.

Half-hidden in the alders, the wolf watched us as we talked. Its face was gray; black streaks outlined its golden eyes. They were already unfocused. The head wobbled as it followed our slightest movements. Hunt began to fill out a capture form. The wolf cocked its ears toward the rustling paper, but its head began to rock, then dropped onto its paws.

Hunt whispered, "Let's go get him. We'll get the trap off, then drag him out here in the open." We crawled into the thicket behind him. He picked up the head and released it. It dropped limply, as though unattached. Hunkering, he took the trap by its springs, put it across his knee, and drew a breath as he pushed down on the springs. When the wolf's jaws relaxed, I gently removed the paw. Feeling up and down the foot, Hunt announced that nothing was broken. In fact, apart from a small cut just above the toes, the paw looked fine. We pulled the limp body out behind us as we backed out of the alders. I smoothed the wolf's fur. It was astonishingly soft. "Sex?" Hunt asked.

I lifted a leg. "Female."

Hunt scribbled on his form, then handed me a bandanna. "Put this over her eyes. Sernylan increases sensitivity to light." I tied the bandanna below her ears. Hunt placed the collar around the wolf's neck, marked the strap with a felt pen, and began to drill holes in the strap with the Yankee screwdriver. "You can put on the ear tags. The pliers are right next to them. Use the first two tags on the string. Should be pretty easy." About an inch long, the ear tags were long, flat Us with the ends sharpened and bent in. They looked awful. "They go on the rear edge, at the base. Just put one in place, grab it with the pliers, and squeeze hard." Glancing at my face, he added, "She can't feel a thing."

I stroked the wolf's left ear. It was softly furred inside and out. It was warm. I took a deep breath, positioned the tag, and squeezed with both hands. The wolf didn't even twitch. I repeated the operation on the other ear, still holding my breath. Now she was a "subject."

"You can get us a pole, thicker than that other one, so we can weigh her," Hunt suggested.

I passed several serviceable saplings, searching for one that was perfect. I found it, bent it as Bert had done, and hacked at the bend with my knife, unused and unsharpened since I'd entered graduate school. It barely cut the bark. I glanced back to see if Hunt and Bert were watching. They were still busy with the wolf. Grunting with effort, I bent the sapling even further and sawed away. Just as I was considering using my teeth like a beaver, the sapling gave, more from my weight than from the knife, and I fell with it into the brush. I twisted and yanked the sapling free, dragged it back, stripped it, and tied one end of the spring scale to its midpoint. Hunt tied the wolf's legs together, then slipped the bottom hook of the scale through the bonds. "Want to guess her weight?" he asked. I remembered a German shepherd about the same size that was close to eighty pounds and guessed seventy. Bert guessed sixty. Bert and I hoisted the pole onto our shoulders so the wolf hung from the scale. Hunt read it. "Fifty," he said, smiling. Bert and I lowered the wolf gently.

Handing me a large syringe with an enormous needle, Hunt asked me to find a vein on a hind leg and get about ten cubic centimeters of blood. I felt beneath the thick fur on the inside of the wolf's lower thigh until I found what I hoped was a vein. I eased the needle in at an oblique angle and slowly drew back on the piston. Nothing. The second attempt also failed, but on the third, bright red blood squirted into the clear plastic cylinder. Following Hunt's directions. I jabbed the needle through the rubber plug of a Vacutainer and watched as the wolf blood was magically sucked in. Hunt asked Bert to retrieve the first syringe from the alder thicket. He checked to make sure it was empty, then pulled a vial from his shirt pocket and filled the syringe, explaining that this injection would be a mixture of penicillin and vitamins to help her recover from the stress of capture. He showed us how to get nipple and canine measurements and record them on the capture form.

The wolf's legs stiffened suddenly. Hunt looked at his watch. "That was a mild convulsion," he said. "If they get more intense or if the intervals between them shorten, I'll give her more Sparine. It prevents convulsions, but I don't want to give her any more drugs than I have to."

The next convulsion was much worse. The wolf gaped, and her stiffened legs jerked at the rope that bound them. Hunt prepared the syringe, and as soon as she stopped thrashing, he gave her a shot in the hip. "She'll be OK now," he said. He rechecked the paw, which was bleeding slightly, decided it didn't warrant a bandage, and filled in the last few blanks on his form.

Bound, blindfolded, and bleeding, punctured, palpated, drugged, weighed and measured, ear-tagged and radio-collared, she lay unmoving amid the syringes, scale, vials, and Vacutainers. I stroked her ears, musing. In her phencyclidine sleep, what dreams might come? She was a hostage to science, but I consoled myself with the thought that she'd soon be free and what we'd learn from her might someday help others of her kind. I was almost completely sure it was worth it.

"What're you going to call her?" I asked.

"The pilots give 'em names but I use the ear tag numbers," he replied curtly. "There are more traps to check. Can you stay here till she moves off? We'll come by in two hours."

"Sure." Hunt and Bert gathered the gear and left me alone with the wolf. I looked down at the tags I'd put on her ears. She deserved better than that. She lived near Upsala Lake, so I'd call her Freya. If I got a chance to call her anything.

I moved Freya into the shade, removed the bandanna, and untied her. She was as limp as a sock, and there was a rasp in her breath that disappeared when I raised her head, so I sat back against a tree with her head in my lap. Clouds sailed overhead, seemingly just above the trees.

An hour later she began to stir. I gently lowered her head to the ground and moved a few yards away to watch. She soon went back to sleep, and so did I. I awoke to a last glimpse of Freya as she staggered away into the alders. I walked down to the road, where a waft of wolf juice told me that the jeep had recently passed. I trotted around a bend. Sure enough, there it was.

As I climbed in, Hunt suggested we visit the two captive wolves he kept near the airport. They might, he said, be of use to Bert and me in our studies of howling and scent marking.

When we arrived at the enclosure, both wolves were frantically pacing back and forth, never taking their eyes off us. Both were larger than Freya. One, russet with bold black markings, must have weighed more than 100 pounds. The other, whose coat was gray and black, was only slightly smaller. As we approached, they raced even faster, repeating a lap that took them around the rear of one large pen, through a doghouse that connected the first pen to a second of similar size, around the rear of the second pen, and back through the doghouse. Every few laps they would enter the doghouse from opposite directions. It seemed that they must collide, but they never did. Hunt hunkered at the fence, and we followed his example. Within a minute the gray wolf had slowed to a rapid walk in the far pen. The red one peered at us from the doghouse, head lowered, unblinking.

Once again I found myself impaled on the gaze of a wolf. I had read that staring was a threat, but I couldn't help myself. I didn't want to break contact. If the red wolf found my regard disturbing, it gave no sign. It came out of the doghouse and sat, still staring. Then its jaw dropped, its tongue lolled, and it gave us a giant doggy grin. It trotted over to us. Hunt slowly extended his hand through the fence. The wolf sniffed it, licked it, and then fell sideways against the fence. Hunt scratched the wolf's flanks through the mesh. Bert scratched its rear. The wolf's eyes closed, its lips relaxed, and it inched slowly forward so Hunt and, a moment later, Bert could scratch every square inch of its flank. I reached through the fence and let it lick my hand, then slowly moved it back to scratch behind its ears. It shuddered slightly and pressed even harder against the fence, which began to bulge ominously. Meanwhile, the gray wolf kept its distance, staying as far away as it could while still keeping us under observation.

Having performed the introduction, Hunt suggested that we go back to the lab for dinner. We stopped at the top of the hill to howl. Hunt climbed out of the jeep, cupped his hands, and produced a bloodcurdling shriek, halfway between a rebel yell and Tarzan's yodel. "That doesn't sound much like a wolf to me," I muttered to Bert.

Hunt overheard me. "Doesn't matter," he replied. As if

on cue the wolves howled back. They didn't sound much like wolves either. Barks, yips, and one hoarse moan were all they could summon. "Sounds as if they need practice," said Hunt, and howled again. This time the wolves did a little better, but not much. He climbed back into the jeep and drove us to the lab. Hunt was still working on his field notes as I staggered off to bed. My dreams began as soon as I shut my eyes. . . .

A sea of fog swirled slowly around a granite archipelago. A wolf padded along a rocky spine, just above the mist. The only sounds were claws clicking on a rock, stomach gurgles, and an occasional harsh sniff. A narrow trail led down into the fog. The wolf sniffed a tuft of weeds, squirted it with urine, and started down the trail. At the bottom of the ridge was a road, ordinarily a place to be wary, but this morning the fog provided cover. Gray dissolved into gray.

The scent hit her suddenly. Her hackles bristled as she lowered her head and advanced slowly, placing each foot carefully. When the odor was within reach, she raised a forepaw and held a perfect point.

When she lowered the foot, the ground gave beneath it, and something bit her just above the paw. She bolted back up the trail, dragging a clanking hook behind her. Even on three legs she cleared a small log easily, but when the hook hit the log, her foreleg was yanked back. She somersaulted onto her back, momentarily breathless. Gasping, she snapped at the chain that held her to the hook, but it was cold and hard and did not yield. After a minute of useless struggle she jumped back over the log. After one more lunge she was able to leave the trail for the shelter of an alder thicket. There she lay, biting again and again

36

at the trap until her lips and gums bled. She kept on biting, sometimes at the trap, sometimes at the alders. Them at least she could break.

The fog fled on the shadows' heels, sunbeams in hot pursuit. She slept until she was wakened by a clatter on the road below. The sound of footsteps came up the trail, crunching in disjointed, two-legged rhythms. Voices filtered through the trees. Suddenly a naked, flat face appeared through the alders. Something stung her haunch. The face receded. She closed her eyes.

When she opened them, the sun had moved. A flat-faced creature sat against a nearby tree, watching. Her paw was free, so she staggered to her feet and plunged deeper into the thicket. She soon found a shady pocket below the roots of a fallen spruce. She turned around in her own length, collapsed, and fell asleep.

It was morning again when she was wakened by a distant drone.

3
Wolf Sign

The prop hauled us along at 120 miles per hour. Freya's signal seemed to come from where we had left her, but Hunt assured me that this was normal. "It always takes them a couple of days to sleep off the drugs," he shouted over the engine's roar. "Then it usually takes a few more days to rejoin the pack." We made a quick loop and moved on to the neighboring Olympus pack before my gorge began to rise.

Hunt always moves fast but never seems to be in a hurry. That morning he was as close to haste as I ever saw him, for he had an appointment in Northton that afternoon. My test was almost over. We circled three more packs, zoomed back to the Forest Service dock, and raced back to the lab, where he grabbed his briefcase, promised to let me know within a week whether he could use me on the wolf project, and was gone. I shouted a quick goodbye to the door as it closed behind him.

I strolled down to the river, where it took me more than an hour to transcribe my notes. The stalest were only twenty-four hours old, but some were already incomprehensible. From time to time I glanced up at the marbled clouds piling up in the east. They looked full of snow to me. The wind came up, and suddenly I was no longer basking but huddling. It was time to get back to Ann Arbor.

I drove through the night and was home before dawn. For the next week I went around in a daze, checking my mailbox after every class for a letter from Hunt. When it finally arrived, I knew without opening it that he had come through. Rejections come in thin envelopes; this one was auspiciously plump, stuffed with federal forms in n-tuplicate. There was even a loyalty oath, which this card-carrying liberal signed without a twinge of guilt. I would have signed anything to join the wolf project.

The rest of the term went quickly, and on New Year's Day, 1972, I left for the wolf project.

Only an Eskimo would have a word for the mixture of sleet, rain, and hail that cloaked my departure in gloom. The rain turned to snow and the snow grew fluffier as I drove north, but as I crossed the Mackinac bridge, the snow was still sticky enough to immobilize the wipers. To stop on the bridge in a blizzard would be suicide—I could hear a semi growling somewhere behind me. I stuck my head out the window and drove like Casey Jones.

I arrived at Ontolagon around 2:00 A.M., grabbed my sleeping bag, and fell into a bunk. Almost immediately, it seemed, I was wakened by the friendly odors of pancakes and coffee. The cook introduced himself as Milo Finnstadt, the wolf project technician. He offered me breakfast, and as I dug in, he passed me the last week's flight sheets. "The Upsala Lake pack should be just south of Birch Road, near the NWCA gate."

39

"NWCA? Northern Women's Christian Association?" I asked.

"National Wild Camping Area. The southern edge is at the end of Birch Road."

I still hadn't the faintest idea what the NWCA was, but I nodded knowingly. Milo offered to accompany me, but I grunted a polite refusal. This would be my first attempt at tracking, and I didn't want any distractions. And though I was reluctant to admit it even to myself, I wanted my first experience with wolf sign to be a private one. Instead, I asked Milo if he'd go out at dusk and drive down Route 3 to Birch Road to pick me up, just in case I came out of the woods far from my vehicle. He nodded and suggested I take the jeep. He explained that he'd just plugged in the tank heater, so it might take a little effort to start it.

Sure enough, the jeep started only with considerable cranking, but soon it settled into an irregular, rattling idle. I got a pair of Green Mountain-style snowshoes out of the garage and checked the recording thermometer as I passed. It was minus 15 degrees Fahrenheit, up 3 degrees from the night's low.

It looked as though Birch Road had been plowed the previous day, but that morning I was the first one on it. The Northland Outward Bound camp was a couple of miles ahead, but the Outward Bounders hadn't been out yet. Four inches of fresh snow provided a perfect medium for tracks but I didn't slow the jeep a bit. With the aid of Murie's *Field Guide to Animal Tracks* I was able to identify most of the tracks that crossed the road: deer, snowshoe hare, red squirrel, and weasel.

I passed the road to Outward Bound and crossed a small stream. Something had come out to the woods, plowing a narrow trench half a yard deep. On the snowbank left

40

by the plow, a knee-level yellow stain marked the place where the trail entered the road. I pulled the jeep over and climbed out to examine the tracks.

Thrown into sharp relief by the oblique rays of the early sun, the prints were startlingly clear. They were hieratic, archetypal signs older than letters or words. Involuntarily I glanced down the road in the direction they headed. My hand fitted neatly in one of the prints. They could be nothing but wolf tracks, but the image of Hunt's skeptical eyebrows reminded me to make sure. I took a receiver and antenna from the jeep. Metal rattled on metal, shattering a silence I hadn't noticed. I flipped the switch, and the air filled with a hiss. With the gain down I tuned for Freya and got a series of faint beeps. Stepping away from the jeep to avoid radio echoes, I pointed the antenna down the road and waved it slowly from side to side. She was north of the road and at the limit of the receiver's range from the ground, at least a mile away. I could follow her tracks without overtaking her and influencing her movements.

I forced myself to move slowly as I folded the antenna and tied it to my day pack, stuffed the receiver inside, and patted my pockets for knife, waterproof matches, and compass. Then I jotted down the time and location. Snowshoes would be unnecessary as long as the tracks remained on the road, so I tied the shoes to my pack next to the antenna and started down the road. Within 100 yards was a large gray scat, a lump of wolf feces, composed mainly of long, coarse white-tipped hair, probably deer. I put part of the scat into a plastic bag and stowed it in an outer pocket of my pack. A splotch of urine marked the snowbank above the scat.

There was no fresh snow in the tracks, and it had been

snowing when I got in around two that morning. I wondered what time the snow had stopped. If I knew, I'd be able to date the tracks to within a few hours. They looked as though they had just been made, but the radio signals told me otherwise.

I scribbled a description of the mark and an estimate of its distance from the first tracks. I could drive down the road and get an exact distance from the odometer later. The road dipped, and halfway up the next hill I could see a black streak in the snow. The wolf had urinated in the road. All the urine lay inside the tracks, and there was a small depression in the snow around the urine. After urinating, she had taken a few steps, then scratched down through the snow with all four paws, sending black dirt halfway across the road. If this was an attempt to cover the other sign, it was ineffective. The earth was directed almost 180 degrees away from the urine.

It was safe to assume that when a wolf raises a leg to squirt a small amount of urine on a target like a snowbank, it is not simply eliminating but is leaving a scent mark. One function of such marks is to advertise the wolf's territory to potential trespassers, and one of my tasks was to determine whether these advertisements simply repel intruders or their effect is more complicated. Scent marks probably have functions besides territory advertisement; they might be involved in the courtship and bonding of mates, for example. My own conjecture was that they might act as mnemonic devices, like blazes on trees, to help wolves find their way. In any case I would need to distinguish between urine clearly used as a mark, like that on the snowbank, and urine simply left on the trail, which might or might not be used as a mark. I decided to call the former raised-leg urinations or RLUs and the latter squat urinations, or SQUs, because it looked as though Freya had squatted as she peed. It looked to me as though the scratching, too, might be a mark, so I recorded it as well.

The wolf had trotted east another quarter of a mile and left another scent mark. After marking the road, she had turned north, heading into dark timber at an oblique forty-five-degree angle.

A quick check with the receiver assured me that I was no closer to Freya than when I had started out. If anything, the signal was weaker. There were interruptions in the sequence of beeps, which meant that she was on the move. The bearing didn't change, but the interruptions became longer, and finally the signal disappeared completely. Even when dawdling, she could do three miles per hour, and though the snow would slow her somewhat, it would slow me more. There was little chance that I'd get close enough to influence her movements. Or vice versa, I thought as I struggled to get the snowshoes on.

Even with snowshoes I sank to my calves on every step; after a few hundred yards I had failed to find a gait that allowed progress at a reasonable rate without requiring frequent pauses for breath. Within ten minutes I was over-heated, but as soon as I stopped, I could feel the chill while sweat trickled down my back. I stowed my parka in my pack, tied my sweater around my waist, and moved on just as my teeth began to chatter. It soon became clear that any speed slow enough to keep my breathing regular was insufficient to keep my body warm. I stopped, put the sweater back on, and tried again.

The wolf trail was an arrow-straight furrow through a world of black and white: looming spruce boughs too dark to be green; then an open birch forest, white trees against white snow. Wolves are color-blind, but here it wouldn't matter. I stopped a moment at the edge of the birch and listened to the forest. Ahead tiny wings fluttered briefly, and off to the right a load of snow whooshed as it slid off a spruce bough and clumphed as it landed. I could smell wet wool, the water proofing on my boots, and the merest traces of spruce. I doubted I could smell a deer an arm's length away. I might be looking at a wolf's world, but I couldn't hear or smell it.

I checked my compass. Freya had not changed course. I jotted down the location and bearing. There had been no scent marks since she'd left the road. Scent marking would be difficult for an animal sunk to its belly in snow, but even when the tracks passed under spruce trees, where the snow was only half an inch deep, there were no yellow stains. The tracks showed clearly, though. Protected from the wind, the four-flamed petals seemed only seconds old, as though time had frozen along with everything else.

Halfway through the birch forest the trail turned abruptly to the right. At the end of this ten-yard excursion, Freya had dug through the snow to the layer of leaves on the ground. The frozen carcass of a long-dead chipmunk lay to the left of the hole, in the center of a small depression where the snow had been packed. A few black-tipped wolf hairs lay in the bowl around the chipmunk. It looked as though she had rolled and rubbed on the chipmunk. She must have been able to smell it ten yards away, buried under almost a yard of snow. I sniffed the tiny corpse. It was pungent but not strong. I scribbled a description of the sign and continued along the wolf trail, once again headed northeast.

After threading her way through an alder thicket, to an old logging road, Freya had left another scent mark, then turned north to follow the road. The topographic map showed no road, but I could deduce my position from the contour lines, which depicted the small knob to my right and the gentle downslope that began just ahead. I dutifully recorded the wolf's latest maneuvers, noting that it was already 10:00 A.M. and that although I had covered only about a mile in three hours, I had already filled six pages with descriptions of signs, distances, and directions.

The going was much easier on the road, where the creaking of my bindings and the crunch of compressing snow were the only sounds. Had Freya known the road was there? Why else would she have plunged straight through those alders? According to some, wolves hunt whenever they travel, and hunting would be much easier from the road. Not only could she see better and move more quietly than in bush, but she could pay more attention to hunting. In bush, every step requires a small decision: under or over, right or left. On the road she could allocate attention to more important matters. There was plenty to attend to; the snow was alive with tracks: snowshoe hare, the prints improbably huge; minute mouse tracks; red squirrel, making a no-nonsense dash from spruce to spruce.

A chickadee fluttered by and landed ahead on a bare spruce bough. I pulled off a glove and sucked the back of my hand to produce a series of squeaks. The chickadee cocked its head but retained its perch. I pulled a salted nut roll from my pocket, put a few peanuts on my hat, and squeaked again. This time the chickadee darted over, hovered noisily, and landed on my head. Its tiny feet and impatient pecks were pleasantly painful, like the insignificant sting of a puppy's teeth. Another chickadee dived in, displacing the first. A third strafed the second, which didn't budge but remained on my head, pecking, even when I began to move on. The other two orbited, chattering. St. Francis of Ontolagon, I said to myself.

I followed Freya down the road another half a mile or so. The trail passed beneath a fallen tree. She had veered around it. That was odd because there was plenty of room beneath the trunk. I detoured around it, then glanced back to see why she had veered. A loop of slender steel cable hung from the fallen tree at the height of a wolf's head. I hadn't seen it from the other side—how had she known it was there? I tapped the snare lightly. The noose slid shut with a deadly hiss. Removing my gloves, I untwisted the wire, stowed the deadly device in my pack, and slogged on.

Freya had left the road to travel along the tops of ridges that paralleled the river. From time to time she had left a ridge to cross a frozen marsh. A moose had meandered through the marsh, before or after the wolf I couldn't tell. Its tracks were joined by another, or perhaps the same moose had made a loop. The wolf trail was lost in the furrow left by the moose. A large yellow stain lay in the trail. Wolf or moose? A quick sniff told me it was the latter. Its piny odor was quite pleasant.

The moose had wandered back and forth, nibbling on a bush here, on a succulent tip there. Its trail was a tangled maze of loops and detours that had obliterated the wolf trail. I circled the marsh, hoping to find the wolf trail where it left. The snow in the marsh was dry and powdery, so it wasn't easy to tell whether any given trail was wolf, moose, or both.

Eventually, however, I found a relatively straight trail headed in the direction Freya had been traveling. There was a spot of urine, unquestionably wolf, where the trail left the marsh. I had been following the trail for almost half an hour when it began to meander in a suspiciously moose-like manner. When the trail led to a young fir the branches of which had been freshly browsed, I began to get worried. Perhaps Freya had been tracking the moose. This faint hope was soon dashed when the trail crossed the thin layer of snow beneath a huge spruce. The only tracks were those made by large cloven hooves. Ever since I'd left the marsh I'd been tracking a moose, not Freya. I ripped a page from my notebook and headed back to the marsh.

I had found the wolf urine on the trail, so she must have backtracked after she had left the marsh. There was no way to verify this, for I had snowshoed over her tracks. I resolved always to walk to the side of tracks I was following, just in case something like this happened again. There was another trail leaving the marsh in a north-easterly direction, and to my relief a snow-covered tuft of marsh grass had been marked with wolf urine. The trail headed up a steep slope that I ascended mainly by brachiation, arriving at the crest winded and sweating profusely.

From the ridgetop I could see that the sun was skimming the treetops. Soon I would have to head for Birch Road if I wanted to get there by dusk. Walking along a plowed road after dark was one thing; snowshoeing through deep snow over rugged terrain, another. I had been averaging about half a mile an hour, and Birch Road was almost a mile away. If I were to allow a half hour margin of safety, I'd have to start back immediately; but the going was easy along the ridge, and it roughly paralleled the road, so I decided to stay on the trail just a little farther. The snow along the ridge crest was windblown and crusty. The tracks were just barely visible.

Freya had walked along the top of a cliff overlooking

an old beaver swamp. On a point that provided a 270-degree view of the swamp, she had lain long enough to melt a circular bowl in the snow. A few wolf hairs remained.

I then headed southeast, along what I hoped was the most direct route to the road. Unfortunately the contour intervals on my topo map were insufficiently fine to delineate the series of miniature cliffs that punctuated the otherwise gently rolling ridges that lay between me and the road. Every few hundred yards I had to decide whether to detour at right angles for some unknown distance in the hope of finding a clear route or to remove the snowshoes, throw them to the top of the cliff, and climb. I alternated these tactics for a while, then decided to detour. The temperature was dropping fast from its high of around zero.

Finally, an hour or so later, I slid down a snowbank onto Birch Road. In the dimming light the road glowed as it wound its way up the next hill, flanked by dark forest. Snowshoes tied to my pack, feet feeling lighter than air, I jogged back to the jeep. I checked my road mileages, found that my estimates were right, then turned back toward the lab.

Hunt's car was in the parking area when I got there. The kitchen was bright and warm. Thick steaks and quartered potatoes simmered on the stove. Hunt was tossing a salad. I'd arrived just in time. The steaks were tender and sweet, more like pork than beef. I asked Milo if they were whitetail.

"No," he replied, "blacktail."

"But blacktails are from the Northwest, aren't they?"

"Not this kind," said Hunt. "This is bear."

"Oh," I nodded sagely.

After dinner as Hunt checked out a rebuilt radio collar, I told him about the day's adventure, leaving out the part about the moose. He agreed that one of my first priorities should be to observe from the air, then to observe the resulting sign from the ground. This way I'd learn how to interpret sign and, more important, learn the limitations of interpretation.

He spread out a map of the Lawrence National Forest and drew the boundaries of several wolf territories. "I'll be here for the next week," he explained. "We'll fly every day, let you watch the packs, then drop off on their trails, let you study the tracks, then pick you up after we've located the other packs. This way you'll get data from as many different packs as possible, which will give you some idea about how much variation there is."

A gray dawn rose reluctantly over Lake Ishpena. It focused its single red eye on the tiny figures inching toward the toy airplane, its silver skis and white wings covered with new-fallen snow. Hunt carried the receiver and antennas, and I carried everything else: cameras; binoculars; sleeping bags; folding saw; lunches; a day pack. We mounted the antennas while Louis drained condensation and topped off the tanks. At twenty below, installing the antennas was a succession of minor horrors. Our gloved hands weren't dexterous enough, so we worked barehanded, leaving small patches of skin frozen to the struts. The wind sock was erect, engorged by a steady twenty-knot breeze from the lake.

The engine roared and the wings bounced at the tips and creaked at the roots as we pounded over rutted snow. Just as it seemed the engine would rip loose on a mission of its own, we leaped into the air, flying through the plume of smoke from the sawdust cone at the east end of the lake.

At 4,000 feet we were in sunlight, but below, the web of frozen lake was dark and occasionally veiled by shreds of cloud. The beeps in my earphones were getting louder. I pointed down, and we skimmed the bottom of the layer of brightly glowing clouds, then broke free. The tops of the spruces on the ridges glowed green-gold, but the valleys were dark.

We found the first pack sprawled like castaways around the wreck of a moose. Except for a pup gnawing a bone held between its paws like a flute, all the wolves were asleep. Ravens hopped among them, pecking at bits of meat. The pup lunged at one bird that got too close, but two flaps of the raven's huge wings lofted it just out of reach, where it hovered while the pup reared and hopped.

The plane's shadow passed over a white-muzzled old wolf. It heaved itself onto its front legs, then onto its rear ones. It soon tired of watching and dropped onto its side. The pup, however, was fascinated. Its head twisted as far to the left as it would go, then snapped around to the right. After a few more orbits the pup began to pace in circles in an attempt to keep us in sight. This tactic was soon abandoned for a better one: By lying on its back, the pup could swivel its head through a full 360 degrees. It was still watching when we flew off in search of wolves that were leaving tracks.

Five vertiginous minutes later we found four, trotting single file along the rocky shore of a long, thin lake. We circled as Hunt filled out his form and I watched for scent marking. "They'll probably mark at the portage," said Hunt. The first wolf was larger than the others, tail high and wagging slightly at the tip. I glimpsed a collar around the leader's neck and asked Hunt about the wolf. "She's an old one," he replied. "About eight." As they approached the end of the lake, the second wolf moved ahead, tail vertical and stiff. It approached a tuft of reeds, sniffed, took two waddling steps forward, then raised its right rear leg. As the old female approached to sniff, the first wolf strode briskly ahead, then scratched the snow, each leg whipping stiffly back in turn as though the wolf were wiping his feet. Black streaks appeared as his paws reached the layer of humus beneath the snow. The wolf that had scratched moved forward. The radio-collared female sniffed the scratches, then squatted briefly. Each of the other wolves sniffed her mark but, as far as I could see, left none of its own. Soon all the wolves disappeared into the thick patch of timber separating the lake from the next one.

Louis held the circle while Hunt and I scribbled furiously. Hunt suggested that I follow the tracks left by the wolves we'd been watching. I agreed eagerly; watching wolves through binoculars was even more discombobulating than with the naked eye. "We'll pick you up around three," he shouted over the engine. "Be back by two, though, just in case." Louis straightened us out with a snap, and we flew out of our circle on a tangent that took us back along the lake the wolves had traversed, over a portage, then over two more long lakes. The wolf trail lay below us on a large lake, about five miles from our circle. Louis made a low pass to check the snow, climbed for his downwind leg, came about, lined us up, and slid to a stop twenty paces from the trail.

I climbed out, breathing deeply in the cold, still air. Hunt handed me my snowshoes, a sleeping bag, a folding saw, and a can of cola. Before I had time to ask, he explained matter-of-factly, "The sleeping bag is just in case

51

you have to spend the night. We're the only people in the world who know where you are, and if we crash, it might take a day or so for a search party to find you. Leave the bag here, and we'll pick it up when we come to get you. See you around three on Russel Lake." I nodded.

"Stay away from the narrows," Hunt shouted as Louis cranked the engine. It caught, and I grabbed my hat as the plane pivoted, spraying me with a prop-blast blizzard. The Cessna roared down the lake, turned into the wind, came back along its tracks, and sprang into the air, buzzing like a gigantic wasp. Soon the buzz faded into an immense stillness. The sky was space dark at the zenith, robin's egg below that, then white at the horizon, where it met a distant snowy ridge.

I thought about Hunt's parting remark as I hoisted my pack and slipped into the snowshoes. If he didn't show up, I wouldn't be able to make it back to the sleeping bag by sundown, but my route was flat and open, so walking after dark would be no problem. I decided that if I had to spend the night, I'd wait till noon the next day, then head southwest. I could probably make it to Winipeg Lake in a couple of days.

I patted my pockets for notebook, knife, compass, matches, candy bars. I carried the bag to the shore, where it would be less likely to blow away. At least I didn't have to worry about its getting ripped off, I thought as I picked up the wolf trail.

I noticed immediately that there seemed to be only three sets of tracks. Where was the fourth? At the east end of the lake I got an answer. The fourth set emerged from the wooded shore and joined the others. I backtracked to see what this one had been up to. The trail meandered through the forest, never getting more than a couple of hundred yards from the shore. I stomped back out onto the lake to scribble. Why had this wolf traveled in the woods when the going was so much easier on the windswept lake? Even if it were a pariah, it could follow at a distance, taking advantage of the trail plowed by the others. There was no pariah anyway; when we watched the pack, they had been traveling together.

I returned to the east end of the lake to find that the wolves had maintained their heading as they plowed through deep powder in a stand of tag alders. They had scent-marked on the first alder they passed. The trail ascended a steep ridge that had probably posed no difficulties for the wolves, but it took me twenty minutes of short traverses to get to the top. The wind had blown the crest almost free of snow. The wolves had turned to the south, taking the easiest route. The trees on the east side of the ridge were tall enough to prevent even a glimpse of the next lake. Nevertheless, the trail veered suddenly to the east, plunged down a steep slope through tall timber, and emerged on a finger of the next lake. Did this mean that the wolves had known the lake was there? Not necessarily. Like yesterday's logging road, the lake might have been only a fortuitous discovery.

The wolves had moved along the northern shore, just far enough out on the ice to take advantage of shallower snow. Once again one of them (the same one?) had taken a difficult route through the deep snow in the forest. I was tempted to follow that trail, too, but I would never make my rendezvous if I did, so I trudged alongside the main trail.

Halfway down the lake the wolves had begun to run. They had fanned out, turned north toward the shore, and joined the tracks of the fourth wolf, also running. They had met three sets of deer tracks. The deer had been running, too, making 4-yard bounds, hooves penetrating to the ice. I backtracked the deer to their beds, about 100 yards in from the shore. The tracks of the fourth wolf passed between two of the beds. The wolf and deer tracks might have been made hours apart, but it seemed likely that the fourth wolf had jumped the deer in their beds and chased them out onto the lake. Now I knew why it had been traveling on the shore.

The deer had headed east along the shore, fanning out. The wolf tracks converged on one set of deer tracks. Where the tracks met was a tuft of gray deer hair, attached to a tiny patch of pink skin. I looked carefully for blood, but there was none. The deer had turned back toward the shore, all four wolves on its trail. The tracks went up a steep bank and into the woods. Half an hour later I had gone only a few hundred yards through a maze of blowdowns, a perfect escape route for the deer, but a nightmare for me and no picnic for the wolves. They had scrambled over, under, and around the obstacles over which the deer had nimbly leaped. Eventually they had given up and turned back to the lake. The deer had escaped with the loss of a tiny patch of hair.

It took me another half hour to get back to the lake. I checked my watch as I caught my breath. This would be my last break if I were to reach the rendezvous on time. At the east end of the lake was an opening through which I could glimpse a much larger lake. As I neared the narrows, I could hear water gurgling beneath the ice. Heeding Hunt's warning, I clambered over rocks rather than risk the thin ice over fast-moving water. The wolves had not been so cautious. One of them had scent-marked a boulder in the center of the strait.

The next lake had pink granite cliffs on both sides. A

frozen waterfall cascaded silently down the one on my right, but I had no time to gawk. I hopped along at double time, with barely a glance at the splendor. I made it to the rendezvous before three, and soon a distant hum announced Hunt's return.

An hour later we were back at the seaplane base, loading our gear into Hunt's wagon. We stopped at Lep's Market on our way through town. While I bought groceries for the next few days, Hunt picked up a large box of meat scraps. I asked if they were for dinner. "Yes, but not ours," he replied. As I should have guessed, we left Route 1 halfway to the lab. We were bringing the meat scraps to the captive wolves. They paced frantically as we approached, as though they knew what was in the box.

Hunt threw a gigantic soup bone into the pen. The red wolf was on top of it as soon as it landed, but the gray one shied away, ran to the doghouse, and peered out at us. We tossed a few more juicy bones into the pen, but the gray wolf refused to emerge. The red one picked each new one up and paraded around with it before dropping it in favor of the next.

We returned to the car and drove on to the lab. I asked Hunt if the wolves had names. "No," he answered, "we just call them the red one and the gray one."

"Since I'll be working with them," I said, "it would be convenient if they had names."

Hunt nodded, eyes on the road.

"Any suggestions?" I asked.

He shook his head.

"How about Red and Gray?" I asked. "That will make it easy to remember which is which."

Again he nodded. A muscle throbbed in his jaw. We drove in silence. Something was left unsaid, but I did not pursue it.

4

The Territorial Interrogative

It had been more than a week since they had killed.

There were no deer in any of the old places, and the moose they had found had stood watching and waiting. After an hour of silent staring the wolves had moved on. That moose was not yet ready to die.

Their leader took them north, past an old kill, where they had gnawed dry and brittle bones. Now they were at the edge of the land they knew. Fresh snow had fallen during the night. It lay knee-deep on the lake ahead. Nevertheless, the big brown male would not relinquish the lead. Even breaking trail for the others, he drew farther and farther ahead. He was heading straight for the foreign shore.

Suddenly he stopped. He sniffed the breeze coming from the nearby trees, then dropped a scat, dry and white from the bones he had chewed. As he moved on, each of the others paused to sniff his scat, then trotted to catch

56

up. The shore was only a few leaps away when the leader's ears went back. He clamped his tail down over his rectum and veered away from the dark forest. The others turned, too, cutting the corner he had made, running to fall in behind him as he skulked along the shore, never taking his eyes from the shadows among the trees.

Again he approached the shore, close enough to smell sweet spruce boughs, but again he froze. He urinated in his tracks like a pup. Time and again he tried to go ashore, but each time the shadows turned him away. Finally, when the pack reached the end of the lake, he plunged into a swampy valley that would take them back to the moose.

I woke the next day at 5:00 A.M. Hunt was out on the porch, wearing work pants he'd pulled on over his long underwear, scanning the sky. "No stars," he said, bringing in a gust of icy air. "I'd better call the flight service." He returned from the phone to say that cloud cover was 100 percent but that Louis thought it would break up. I hastily washed down some cookies with scalding coffee and followed Hunt out to the station wagon. An hour later we were in the air. Life on the ground was becoming an interlude.

The overcast was complete, but we had our own private sunrise as we skimmed an endless prairie of gray. When the sun rolled up under the right wing, the brumous terrain turned to butterscotch ripple, but I was too busy to enjoy the colors that slid silently beneath the skis. We were close enough to the clouds that for once I could see how fast we were going. Our velocity lent urgency to my search for a signal.

I had the gain up as far as I could without risking permanent damage to my ears. The hissing in the headphones drowned out the engine. Hunt claimed to be hard-of-hearing; I wondered if he'd spent too many hours with the gain up, too many days in noisy airplanes, or both. When sunbeams began richocheting around the cabin, I risked nausea by shutting my eyes to concentrate on imaginary beeps, trying to tell them from the real ones.

After about ten minutes I clicked the receiver off and passed it to Hunt, whose patience, I assumed, must be wearing thin, though he had given no sign. Within two minutes he'd found the wolf and we were spiraling down through the clouds. The layer was thick, but soon we caught hazy glimpses of a solid world of wooded ridges and snowy lakes. A pack of five was asleep on the shore of a small lake, gray coins that I would never have thought were wolves had they not been the only objects without a coating of snow. They were evenly spaced, each wolf about five yards from its neighbors, not huddled together as I would have expected. I jotted down their location, and we left without disturbing them.

As we began to climb back into the clouds, I noticed a wavy line along the shore of a lake to the north. It disappeared as I reached for my binoculars, so I dismissed it as a trick of light. The sun was poking through over there, and it could have been the shadow of the tree line. I kept looking, though, and it reappeared. Hunt had seen it, too, and motioned for Louis to take us over. It was no shadow—the trail of a meandering moose, perhaps, or of a pickled snowmobiler. I mentioned these possibilities to Hunt.

"No," he replied over his shoulder. "Wolf." How he knew that I'll never know. We were still a mile away, and every set of wolf tracks I'd ever seen was laser-straight, no-nonsense, A to B, not like this crazy oscillation. "That's Border Lake," Hunt informed me. I found it on my map as we flew over. It was two and a half miles long and half a mile wide at the southwest end, a little narrower at the northeast, which lay about a mile from the Canadian border.

Our second pass took us lower, and I could see that the wavy line was a trail made by several animals through deep snow. I still couldn't be sure the animals were wolves. The trail crossed the lake at the northeast end and moved along the long northwestern shore, repeatedly approaching to within a few yards of the forest, then swinging back onto the lake. After a mile or so of this vacillation, the trail turned back south across the lake.

"Can we land here?" I asked Louis, who replied by dropping a wing and sideslipping down to about 100 feet. He examined the surface as we rushed along, then grunted and asked around his cigar where I'd like to be dropped. "Whichever end is easier. Downwind, I guess."

While Louis trimmed for landing, Hunt informed me that there were two radioed wolves in the nearest pack, but since Border Lake was at the northern edge of their territory, the tracks could just as easily have been left by their unradioed neighbors to the north. He recommended that I get an accurate count of the number of wolves that had made the tracks. If there were six, the chances were good that the tracks had been left by the residents. He couldn't pick up a signal, so they weren't anywhere near. We took some pictures on our downwind leg, and the landing was uneventful. Once again Hunt provided me with a sleeping bag, a folding saw, and a can of cola.

Buffeted by the blizzard of the turning Cessna, I strug-

gled into my snowshoes. I shouldered my pack and plod-
ded alongside the tracks. They were wolf all right, heading
the same way I was, so I was seeing what they had seen,
more or less. I crouched to lower my point of view. Everything looked the same—a quarter of a mile of open snow
and a line of spruce on the opposite shore. There was one
deep trail and a shallower one to the right, signifying at
least three wolves. Then the deep trail split, and one fork
split again. The other folk was deeper, so there had to be
at least five. Or, I reminded myself, one wolf could have
crossed the lake five times, but that possibility was sufficiently unlikely to be dismissed. The trails merged as
the wolves had once again formed a single file. One of
the wolves had gone to within two yards of the northern
shore but had turned back, leaving a scat and a sprinkle
of urine at its apogee. The other tracks also approached
the shore, but each turned back at a different distance,
leaving another five sets of tracks, so it probably was the
resident pack.

I stopped to sketch the tracks and reconstruct the scene.
The wolves had been traveling single file. If they were a
few yards apart when the leader turned back, each wolf
would cut the corner he had made at a different point,
leaving six nested parabolas in the snow.

This conjecture did not, however, explain why the lead
wolf had turned back in the first place. Could he have
heard a howl? Smelled a foreign scent? There was only
one way to check. I spent the next two hours cutting
transects through the trees and brush on the shore. I found
no sign, but that meant nothing. An inch of snow would
conceal scent marks from the eyes of a human but not
from the nose of a wolf. When I returned to the lake, the
wind was still, so I tried a series of howls. A reply would

have told me another pack was near, but there was no reply. That, too, meant nothing. Though it was unlikely that the tracks were more than a few hours old, a pack traveling at average speed, five miles per hour, could be far, far away by now.

I returned to the trail and counted thirteen separate approaches to the shore. Four more of these approaches were marked with urine. Thirteen times the pack had nearly gone ashore. Thirteen times the wolves had turned away. A clear depiction of what psychologists call approach-avoidance conflict had been inscribed in the snow, a paradigm of territorial behavior.

After the last withdrawal the wolves had headed south, back toward the center of their territory. I followed them through a marsh and over a low ridge, then returned to the lake to wait for Hunt. I dusted snow from a rock, sat, and drew a sketch of the tracks in case the photographs didn't come out.

When the sketch was complete down to the last urine stain, I munched a peanut butter sandwich, sipped the cola, and enjoyed the silence. The temperature couldn't have been much above zero, but the air was still and dry, and the clouds had moved toward Lake Superior to regroup. There was enough energy coming off the lake to give me a sunburn. From my perch on the rock I could see the whole length of tracks. Suppose it was this quiet when the wolves had crossed the lake. Suppose the only sound was the crunch of snow beneath their enormous paws. Suppose there were no howls from the north, no scent marks either. Suppose it was not other wolves that had turned them back, but their own knowledge of their territory, of where they were.

"Heresy," I muttered.

Suddenly there was a rush of wind behind me, and a huge shadow swept across the snow. I jumped off the rock, tripping over my snowshoes, which I hadn't bothered to remove. On hands and knees I looked up to see a yellow Cessna glide by, only twenty yards away. The pilot's face was clearly visible as he waved. The engine exploded into full power, yanking the plane into the sky, but it barely made it over the trees. It buzzed away to the north, leaving me wondering what *that* was all about. Whoever it was had shattered my Wilderness Experience and caused me to spill my cola as well. Silence had returned to the lake, so I drained the unspilled dregs as I tried to soak up the solitude along with the sunlight, but the stillness was different now, contaminated with the barnstormer's intrusion.

On the flight home I shouted a query about my guest. "Gresh," replied Hunt and Louis in unison. Hunt went on to explain that Gresh's maneuver was not the gratuitous prank it seemed but rather a legitimate exercise of his authority as a local guardian of law and order.

"You mean he's some kind of cop?" I asked, my voice an incredulous octave higher than normal.

"Sure is," said Louis. "He's one of a few flying game wardens working this part of the state. Hope you weren't doing anything illegal."

"What kind of crime could I commit alone on a frozen lake?" I asked—a little too innocently, I thought, but they let it pass.

"You could be running a gigline, or poaching deer, or snaring wolves, for example. He's busted plenty of guys doing all those things with those dead-stick glides of his." I asked what a gigline was and learned that it was an illegal fishing technique, in which a coat hanger or similar device was used to set the hook automatically. Louis's instructions on how to make one were suspiciously detailed.

The reference to snaring wolves reminded me of the radioed wolf we'd located in the bed of the pickup in Gantry.

Hunt explained that the poacher had walked. "Couldn't touch him," he explained. "He said he'd shot it outside the national forest. Until we get better legal protection there's not a thing we can do unless we can prove the wolf was taken in the forest. We got the collar back, though."

The next week was an old-time movie, a jerky frenzy of sped-up processions and excursions. We'd be up at five, in the air by six, down again by noon, eating lunch on the road if at all. The time we spent on the road provided our only opportunity to relax. I gradually took over the driving and let Hunt do the talking as his eyes scoured the woods for wildlife. I learned quite a bit about his wife, Charlotte, and their four children, but nothing about where Hurricane was. His affection for Charlotte was obvious. Twice that week he told of driving slowly through his neighborhood as he overtook an unusually attractive woman, only to find himself leering at his own wife.

As the breeding season approached, in late February, the tempo of wolf behavior accelerated. As we tried to keep as many packs as possible under observation, our behavior sped up too. Every day I'd track a different pack— sometimes two, and the landings and takeoffs became a blur.

Staggering into the lodge exhausted and ravenous after a day on snowshoes, I'd cook up whatever poor road-killed creature I'd found during the day (there was no time for shopping), shower, and transcribe my notes, often as not falling asleep over them. Daylight was too precious for anything but tracking, so I finished them before dawn.

My schedule left little time for reflection on what, if anything, the data I was gathering meant. Only when weather prevented flying was I able to ponder the issues with which I'd begun. Did Freya know where she was going, or did she wander aimlessly from one herd of deer to the next? It was going to be difficult to develop criteria sensitive enough to discriminate purpose from wandering which were also objective enough to satisfy Hunt and the Bachs. And if I could develop such criteria, what would my results tell us about the naked wolf? The more I learned about wolves, the less they seemed like people. It was with mixed feelings that I realized that I was adopting some of Hunt's objectivity. Nevertheless, I continued to refer to the wolves not by number but by name.

One afternoon in mid-February, I followed a wolf trail that led me over a series of portages connecting a series of short lakes—slow going but perfect for my purposes. The few miles of tracking I'd already done had made it quite clear that raised-leg urinations (RLUs) were rare on frozen waterways, probably because there were no vertical targets to squirt at. In order to be sure that marking rates were lower on lakes when other factors were held constant, I planned to follow segments of tracks that included roughly equal distances on lakes and land in the same regions. The day's tracking did not falsify my hypothesis. All the scent marks were on the portages. The discovery wasn't exactly earth-shaking, but it was the first generalization I'd been able to test.

The pack had traveled single file, trotting straight across

six small lakes. In deep snow, a single file conserved energy, as the leaders broke trail for the others. Like cross-country skiers, wolves often rotated the lead. They were likely to travel single file even when the snow wasn't deep, from force of habit, I supposed. On the seventh lake the wolf trail split, then split again. One wolf had entered the woods on the north shore, two others had cut through a swamp to the south, and the remaining two had traveled on the lake, leaving trails about four yards apart. It took me an hour to follow the single trail along the north shore, an hour to backtrack the pair that had stayed on the lake to the point where they had split, and another hour and a half to follow the pair that had gone through the swamp. By mid-afternoon I was ready to leave my cap to the next branch that took it.

With all this backtracking, the entire day's work would cover only about two and a half miles, a distance I'd walked three times. I bitterly recalled the 3,000 hours of observations on which George Schaller had based his *Serengeti Lion*. If I assumed an overall average rate of wolf travel of two miles per hour, it would take me 2,400 days like this one to acquire equivalent amounts of data.

The wolves had traveled single file across the next portage, scent-marking profligately. How could they make enough urine? Perhaps they used less on each shot than it seemed. I made a note in the margin of my notebook to try to simulate a typical urine stain with measured amounts of colored liquid on different kinds of snow. The day's tracking had already filled six pages of notebook with descriptions of routes, separations, rejoinings, distances, and scent marks. The quantity was reassuring.

All thoughts of data recording evaporated when I reached the next lake. Ahead the tracks showed that the wolves had fanned out, running. The trail of a running deer lay across the lake, joined by the wolf tracks, which swung to intercept it. For once the sign could be interpreted unambiguously: The remains of the deer lay on the shore. I veered to the left, so as not to obliterate any sign. There wasn't much left of the deer; a small piece of hide, a spine, and a rumen lay in the center of an arena of packed pink snow dusted with gray-brown deer hair. Though intact, the spine had been gnawed clean enough for museum display. There wasn't a shred of meat on it.

Hunt had asked that I collect a jaw and a long bone for any kills I found. The jaws provide teeth, which could be sectioned to determine the victim's age: one layer of dentin for each year. The marrow of long bones would provide information about the animal's general physical condition—healthy ones have plenty of fat. A classic study in the sixties had shown that wolves on an island in Lake Superior were usually highly selective, killing moose that were very young, very old, or in poor shape. Hunt was interested in seeing to what extent the same was true of wolves and deer on the mainland, where the deer population seemed to be declining.

Glad for once to be able to do something for Hunt, I circled the area, but found no bones. I then trudged in a spiral, and on my third gyre I found a mandible. I found no longer bones, but on my fifth orbit I found five circular depressions in the snow, each with a few gray wolf hairs frozen into the bottom: beds. That meant that they probably hadn't carried the bones away but had crunched them up and devoured them.

The sun was in the treetops, and it was still a mile or so to the rendezvous, so I reluctantly left the wolf trail and took the most direct route. I got there just in time.

There was no plane in sight, but I could hear it droning to the south. The engine noise peaked about every thirty seconds, so I knew Hunt and Louis were circling. They were probably watching the pack I had followed.

The engine noise faded, and just as I was beginning to wonder if I was waiting on the right lake, the Cessna appeared at the other end, already on its final approach. The lake was small, and the plane zoomed by less than twenty-five yards away, showering me with snow from the prop blast. It seemed to have barely enough room to stop. Louis spun it around, taxied back, and stopped with the left wing tip just over my head. To my surprise, Hunt was not in the plane. As I loaded my pack and snowshoes into the cargo compartment behind the rear seat, Louis explained, "No way we can take off from this little lake with three people on board. Doc's waiting for us on the next lake over."

I took the front seat and strapped myself in. "Fact is," Louis continued, "with the snow this soft, we'll be lucky to get out of here at all." The engine roared as we taxied to the downwind end of the lake. "If we're not in the air by the time we pass that cliff, we won't be able to clear the trees at the end of the lake."

"We'll be able to stop in time, though, won't we?"

"I doubt it," he replied.

I remembered that the leading cause of death among wildlife scientists was crashes in light planes. The plane surged ahead, but more sluggishly than usual. As I remembered, with skis the plane took off at about seventy knots. I kept my eyes glued to the airspeed indicator, trying not to look at the wall of trees at the end of the lake. When we passed the cliff, the dial read forty. Suddenly the trees were very close. They seemed to grow taller as we rushed toward them. The airspeed indicator read fifty-five. Suddenly we broke free of the slushy snow. We still weren't climbing, though. The trees loomed. I thought about the high-octane gasoline in the tanks overhead and glanced at Louis. When I saw his face, I reached for the door handle. His jaw was clenched, and the eye I could see was closed tight. "This is it," he muttered. I ducked as low as the seat belt would permit and wrapped my arms around my head, bracing for the crash. Suddenly I felt the plane bank. The moment of impact passed without so much as a snipped twig. I peeked over the instrument panel to see a previously invisible arm of the lake extending ahead of us for more than half a mile.

One look at Louis told me that he'd known about the arm all along. He was grinning, and both eyes were open now, twinkling, as he said, "Lucky for us that lake had that dogleg in it, huh?" I sat back and pretended to enjoy the joke, resisting the temptation to ask how many times he'd taken off from that particular lake and how many other rubes had actually ducked under the dash. I was afraid to hear the answer.

By the time we picked Hunt up and took off once more, I had thought up four different forms of revenge. From the glances Hunt and Louis exchanged, it was clear that Hunt was the author of the joke.

An hour after we had landed, Hunt was on his way to the University, shouting that he'd be back in a few days, for the beginning of the breeding season. In the wake of his departure the silence of the lodge was almost oppressive. I pulled a chair up to the fireplace and thumbed through some basic references on wolf behavior.

I felt that I'd earned a break, so in order to make some sense out of what I'd learned about wolves and in the hope of relating it to naked ones, I hauled out my box of books and articles on wolf behavior. I began with Rutter and Pimlott's *The World of the Wolf* because it had lots of good pictures and some tantalizing diagrams of what might have been coordinated hunting strategies but which might also, as Rutter and Pimlott point out, have only been good luck.

Next I turned to Devra Kleiman's excellent monograph on scent marking in the dog family, which when combined with the little I'd already found out by tracking, raised many more questions than it answered. If RLUs were territorial displays, why did wolves produce them not only along borders but throughout their territories? Did this mean that scent marks were sometimes landmarks? Why do wolves, both male and female, mark more often in the breeding season? Why do they sometimes scratch the ground after marking?

Obviously I would have to learn more about the social life of wolves. According to many of the accounts I read, including Adolph Murie's classic *Wolves of Mount McKinley* the popular view of packs as organized along rigid lines of dominance was not the whole story; the dominant breeding pair, called the "alphas" are the focus of warm, often ecstatic, love and devotion.

Alphas do often impose their will on other wolves, though. They are usually male, bigger, stronger, and more energetic than most other wolves. The classic descriptions of pack structure by Konrad Lorenz, Rudolph Schenkel, and others emphasize the role of dominance and describe wolves as living in a rigid dominance heirarchy, or pack order, in which privilege is ascribed strictly on the basis of rank. The emphasis on dominance by German ethologists may be attributed in part to the fact that their studies were based entirely on captive wolves; that is like studying human social structure by observing behavior in prisons—another environment in which, perhaps not coincidentally, dominance determines the quality and outcome of most encounters. Other conclusions about pack society, on the other hand, were based almost entirely on the aerial observations of free-ranging wolves, and they implied that alphas lead not only because they are feared but also because they are loved.

The love that binds members of a pack to the alpha and to one another is celebrated in an excited rally called a group ceremony, in which wolves swarm around the alpha, jostling one another as they try to lick his muzzle amid barks, yips, and an occasional growl. The group ceremony is one of several behaviors peculiar to wolves (and their domestic cousins, dogs) that organize a pack into an efficient, coordinated hunting team. Scent marking and howling are other such integrative behaviors. In fact, almost every species-specific behavior seen in wolves is somehow implicated in the maintenance of amicable relations among intimate killers.

Sometimes, however, the center cannot hold, and like a neutron fleeing a nucleus, a wolf leaves its pack and wanders alone. Lone wolves are the exception rather than the rule in this highly social species and the processes which culminate in a wolf setting out on its own were subject to debate. One view, championed by Michael Fox, had it that a lone wolf is one genetically destined to be an alpha, who cannot tolerate an inferior position and who leaves the pack voluntarily. On the other hand Young, in The Wolves of North America, states that lone wolves are those too old to hunt with the rest of the pack.

Since lone wolves use scent marks neither as tokens of

affiliation nor as signs of ownership, their scent marking should differ in interesting manners from that of wolves in packs. I was anxious to see if lone wolves scent-marked at all and, if possible, to figure out how they were able to trace territory boundaries with such accuracy. If they were nomads, with no knowledge of the terrain through which they roamed, but could identify territorial boundaries by "reading" scent marks or hearing howls, then so could the residents. Since lone wolves provided a chance to see if mental maps were necessary, I was obliged to pursue them. This was how science was supposed to work, by the elimination of alternative explanations.

The first step was, of course, to find some tracks, so the afternoon after Hunt's departure I flew in search of Amy, a lone female that was last located a few miles south of Axe. We were using Transbush Airways, a local charter service, and my pilot was Sam Stein, the owner. Like Louis, Sam lived by the adage that there are old pilots and bold pilots, but no old, bold pilots. Moreover, since Sam's background was in charter flying rather than in slurry bombing, his style was much gentler than Louis's, so radio tracking with him was more enjoyable than with Louis.

The weather was marginal, and Sam warned me that we might have to land at any moment, but I got Amy's signal as soon as we were airborne, so I told him we'd be done in a few minutes. I missed her on the first pass and signaled for a 180. Sam completed the turn but said that he wanted to land while he could still see the lake. He had a point. The ceiling was coming down fast. Nevertheless, I could still see trees 1,000 feet below. There was a skin of rime on the leading edges of the struts, but the wings looked clear, and the tachometer showed normal

71

revs, so the prop wasn't icing yet. "Just let me get close enough to spot her tracks," I begged.

Sam shrugged and trimmed for descent. The signal came from behind us again. We did another 180. By the time we'd completed it, I could no longer see the ground. Tendrils of mist flew past. It was getting dicey, but I finally got the small crescendo that meant we were over her, and I signaled for a circle on the right, so I could scan the ground. There was no ground to scan. Sam spiraled down to 500 feet, and we could barely see the trees. Three hundred feet. Now the signal came in stronger on the left antenna. There was something funny in the beeps, a fuzziness I'd never heard before. We circled on the left, maintaining our altitude as the ceiling dropped over us like a cloak. "That's it," said Sam. "We're going home."

Before I could acknowledge the wisdom of his decision, a bright red glow suddenly filled the mist dead ahead. "Left! Left!" I screamed, but Sam had already stomped in full left rudder and yanked the yoke in his lap with one hand while he punched in full throttle with the other. The stall horn howled, and the whole airframe creaked with the strain. The right wing tip missed the WAXE radio transmitter tower by two yards. I had homed in on an echo off the tower. Sam glanced over, grimacing. The corners of his mouth were drawn down, and the cords of his neck stood out.

"*Now* can we go home?" he asked.

It looked a little clearer ahead, so I pleaded for one more minute. I had the true signal, dead ahead, on the snow-covered fairways of the Axe Country Club. And there she was, trotting along between the third and fourth holes, looking like a furry German shepherd. If I hadn't seen the collar, I wouldn't have believed she was a wolf, so casually did she move—not furtively, not sneakily, looking neither left nor right, just trotting along, heading straight for downtown Axe. "Let's go in," I said. "I've got some tracks to follow."

"Bring your clubs," said Sam with a smirk.

On the way to the golf course it occurred to me that it might be interesting to see what Amy did when she hit town. There wasn't really enough light left for tracking, and she'd be making new ones tomorrow. Besides, this was one time when it would be permissible to get close to a wolf on the ground. Although the sleet and resulting premature dusk had imposed a curfew on pedestrians, there were a few cars enthusiastically clanking their tire chains on the slushy streets. Since anyone might see her, I rationalized, it might as well be me.

The beeps came in strongest in a neighborhood of white frame houses with recently shoveled walks a few blocks northeast of Axe High. She was so close that I could get the signal even with the antenna disconnected. It was time to go on foot. It would have been convenient to leave the antenna in the truck, but I needed it to determine the direction of the signals. A dog went wild behind the nearest house, so I ran around the corner into an unplowed alley. A husky mix was straining at its chain, lunging toward the far end of the alley. A set of wolf-sized paw prints led that way.

By the time I got to the end of the alley, the signals were perceptibly weaker. I took a bearing from the end of the next block and began to run. She was straight ahead. The soggy snow was falling more heavily, gray with soot before it landed. At the end of the next block there was a shout, a slam, and a curse from just around the corner. I skidded to a stop and clicked on the receiver. Suddenly

73

a bass voice behind me nearly made me drop the antenna. "You lookin' fer yer doag?" it said. I whirled to see an enormous hunched creature. I shuffled two steps to the left to put a piece of ice between us and acknowledged that I was indeed looking for my dog, adding, in case he wondered about the antenna, that I was less than satisfied with the performance of the shock collar I had just purchased at an outrageous price.

The man informed me that my dog had just crossed Taconite, the main street of Axe, and was headed north, toward the open-pit mine. With visions of Amy slipping off the edge and falling to her death, I shouted my thanks and sprinted for the truck, clutching the receiver under my arm like a football. I was halfway down the alley when I heard the man's parting remark booming out behind me: "Hey, sonny, you ought to feed that dog better."

When I reached the mine, the signals were already coming from the northeast. She had evidently gone around it, so I drove to Windy Point, where Transbush Airways was based. The point provided a convenient place from which I could monitor her movements. I hoped for her sake that she would continue north and not again succumb to the attraction of Axe. What could those attractions be? I wondered as I huddled in the cab between bearings. Wolves fear people even more than people fear wolves, and with greater justification. One attraction might be the male dogs of Axe, for the breeding season was near and wolf-dog matings were not unheard of. Following her trail might tell me if she was in heat, for when wolves come into estrus, uterine blood can be seen as a pink tinge in their urine and sometimes as red drops on the snow.

Using the jeep, I homed in on Amy's signal in the morning. As I had hoped, she had overcome the allure of Axe and continued north along Mink Trail. Her signal came from a point too near the road for me to risk following her. The last thing I wanted to do was chase her back toward Axe.

Instead, I spent the rest of the day following Freya. It was a day I would never forget, for it was on that day that I first glimpsed the dance of the wolves.

5

Dance
of the Wolves

The dance begins slowly. As the earth precesses into wolves' sexual season, the sun strikes the north longer every day. Pineal glands pick up the rhythm, sending steroids to the adrenals and gonads and back. Helical acids writhe as eggs and sperm are spawned. Testes throb; nostrils quiver. Uterine blood stains the snow.

Freya was showing blood. Beneath her tail the fur was dark and matted, and she left a trail of pink, dime-sized disks as she moved slowly through deep new snow. There were deer in the narrow valley where she hunted, so she stopped often to listen and sniff; when she did, she left a larger stain. Hoofprints and pellets were everywhere, and in the still dawn air deer scent lay in every hollow. She marked every boulder and snow-covered log she passed, raising a leg to spray a few drops of bloody urine.

Pungent deer scent filled the air; the whitetails were very near. Her last meal, an unwary hare she had killed the day before, had been small. Her strides grew longer, but the powdery snow muffled their sound. Suddenly she stopped, her stiffened forelegs driving deep into the snow as she lifted her nose to test the air. Her bowels loosened, and she left a brown, watery smear. She was not the only wolf in the valley.

Fast footsteps crunched close behind her. She leaped onto a snow-covered boulder and crouched, ready to spring.

He trotted down the snow-packed road, legs paddling loosely. His tail swayed easily from side to side but never strayed far from vertical. The sun was warm, the sky clear, and his belly full. He had just finished a deer; now he was ready for another. As he passed one of his marks, he veered to savor the familiar odor. He cocked a leg, added a squirt of urine, and underlined his mark with a scrape of one hind leg. He sniffed once more and padded on. A moment later he raised his leg again.

There had been many deer in the herd he'd jumped the night before. He found another mark, one he'd left just before the kill. Absently he squirted again, now intent on the odor of deer. So complete was his concentration that the new scent took almost a second to register. He skidded to a stop, snorted, and tasted the air.

He shoved his nose into the tuft of weeds that broadcast the wonderful aroma. He snorted, slurped, and buried his nose in the snow beneath the weeds, then ran back and forth along the road, sniffing for tracks. He whimpered as he ran.

Tendrils of female scent lured him off the road onto a trail that wound down into a deep, narrow valley where the scent was even stronger. On the trail the sweet odor was clear, and he ran with his nose to the snow, ignoring the scent of deer that grew stronger after every turn. Sud-

77

denly her tracks were gone. In his haste he had overshot her turnoff. He planted his feet, whirled, backtracked. Once again he ran past the rock where Freya sat watching his blunders with narrowed eyes. Then her quiet "woof" told him his search was over.

He approached the rock slowly, pausing after every step. She rose onto all four feet, hackles bristling. She was an impressive sight as she stood above him, lips curled back from her fangs. He approached to within a body length of the rock, sat, and gazed up at her, lower jaw hanging in a panting grin. Warm and heavy with freshly digested meat, his breath rose to her nostrils. Freya's hackles dropped minutely. Her lips relaxed.

The male rose, took one more step, and reared slowly, almost delicately, onto his hind legs, supporting himself with a foot placed gingerly on the edge of her rock. She growled softly but showed no teeth. She sniffed his foot and gave it a quick, tentative lap. Slowly the male straightened his legs, bringing his nose to hers. Freya's growls were soft and constant, almost a purr. Their noses touched. Her breath was ripe but bore the sour smell of prolonged hunger. He snorted, dropped onto all fours, and turned onto the trail, where deer scent hung like fog. He heard the crunch of her landing, but he was already concentrating on the hunt. Once past the place where he had turned around, he found fresh tracks. He shot a quick glance over his shoulder to see if she was following. She was. He began to run.

Their racket startled a sleeping doe. Had she stayed where she was, she might have been safe, for she was well off the trail and there were other deer ahead, but she leaped to her feet, eyes bulging with fear, and bounced toward the trail. Seeing her mistake, she whirled, but it was too late. The wolves were already charging. The male bit into a haunch and held on, allowing Freya to seize the soft skin of her belly. There was no pause between the killing and the meal. Freya pulled off a foreleg and carried it a short distance to devour it away from the eyes and mouth of the other wolf; he sat quietly, watching her eat. Soon she had stripped the leg to the bone, and she returned to the carcass, where the other wolf had begun to gorge. She could tell by his scent that he was a male, but as she approached to sniff his rear, a growl sent her to the other end of the carcass, where she pulled off the other foreleg. This one she did not carry quite so far.

Sated, the male flopped down for a nap. Freya moved in, chewing away at the tender strips of meat that lay on either side of the spine. When she finished, she napped, too. The sun was high. When they rose, they returned to the carcass and gnawed every piece until it was clean and white and until only the skull, spine, and femurs remained. The smaller bones were crushed, chewed, and swallowed. Then they left, traveling side by side a few yards apart, working their way up a cliff that provided a view of the valley. Once again they went to sleep, this time only a yard apart. When they left their beds late that night, they left one trail, not two, and their scent marks were in pairs—one sinusoidal, yellow, and crisp; the other a spray, orange, and diffuse. Freya's dance had begun.

I picked up Freya's signal from Jack Pine Trail and drove north until I found where she had crossed October Lake Road. Her signal was strong, so I backtracked to the west. When I returned to the truck for a late lunch, the signal had faded, so I followed her trail east. For once the record was unambiguous. She had been joined by another wolf. Its tracks were half again as large as hers, and its scent marks were much different from hers in both form and color. They had jumped a deer and killed it almost immediately. I followed their trail, recording several pairs of scent marks. I was certain that the new wolf's scent marks were typically male, but I hadn't yet seen Red or Gray raise their legs, so I couldn't be sure. I made a note to examine their marks when and if they ever did. On the way out to the road I picked up the deer skull and femur for Hunt.

The phone was ringing as I entered the lodge. It was Hunt calling to see how things were going. "Uh-huh's" gave way to "golly's" as I told him about Freya's suitor. Since one of his major interests was in how packs are formed, he was anxious to have me confirm her liaison and asked that I fly in the morning in an attempt to see them from the air. While I was up, he continued, I might as well locate a few packs to the northeast of Axe.

Stars still shone in the clear western sky as Sam and I rocked the struts to free the skis from the ice; by the time the first sliver of sun appeared, we were at cruising altitude. We located Hunt's wolves without difficulty, and soon we were homing in on Freya's signal in a straight, shallow descent, the beeps exactly the same on both antennas. Sam and I saw her at the same instant. She was directly ahead, asleep with another wolf, larger and much darker than she, on a ridge overlooking their kill. On our second circle the larger wolf slowly got to his feet, stretched, and walked over to her. He lowered his snout as though to touch noses but suddenly jumped back and sat down. Freya rose slowly, stretching first her front legs and then her rear ones. With almost feline languor she walked slowly past the male wolf, drawing her tail across his muzzle.

When the other started after her, however, she whirled. Once again the dark wolf jumped back, then swaggered over to a nearby rock and raised a leg. Freya sauntered to the rock and followed suit. The dark wolf sniffed the rock and lifted his leg again. For more than a minute the two wolves circled the rock in each other's tracks, barely breaking stride to sniff and cock their legs. Then Freya frisked away, leaping into the air as though chasing a bug, presumably an imaginary one, given the paucity of airborne insects at twenty below zero. In any event, whether her antics were play or ploy, their effect was not only to break the circle but to give her the last squirt.

The darker wolf also began to romp, running in a precessing family of ellipses with Freya at one focus, pausing from time to time to drop onto extended forelegs in a kind of canine bow, always directed toward Freya, who remained seated, turning her head to follow his erratic orbit. After half a dozen circuits her consort slowly approached her from behind and nuzzled her rear. She whirled and snapped, sending her companion slinking off to glance over a shoulder as he sat and licked the injured flank. Freya trotted over, touched her snout to the other's mane, and then loped off along the ridge, the other wolf close behind. Within a minute they disappeared into a dense forest of spruce.

In the field notes I scribbled as we circled, I scrupulously refrained from referring to the new wolf as "he," for I could almost hear Hunt, my mild-mannered superego, politely inquiring how I had determined the new animal's sex. Nevertheless, I could not help thinking of her companion as male. A week or so later, when Sam and I once again homed in on the pair from the northeast, male was exactly what he proved to be.

As we flew over the north shore of October Lake with

the signal loud and clear, I noticed a curious pattern on the snow-covered ice. We swooped for a better look. Two sets of wolf tracks formed a series of connected loops, as though some gigantic Palmer penman had loosed his wrist in preparation for cursive script. At the end of the tracks were two wolves, locked rear to rear, pivoting about each other as they made their way slowly toward the safety of the shore. They must have tied out on the lake, where they would be easy prey to the first armed snowmobiler or ice fisherman who saw them. We climbed quickly to watch for potential visitors and to avoid disturbing the wolves.

"How come they get stuck like that?" Sam asked.

"There's a gland on the penis that swells and muscles in the vagina that tighten," I replied.

Sam wasn't satisfied. "Not 'How?' Why?" he asked.

There he had me, for the library work I'd done in the fall had revealed that the mechanics of sphincters and glands, but not their functions, are understood. Ties can last for up to half an hour, and semen flows the whole time, but why wolves take half an hour to accomplish what most mammals do in a few seconds remains a mystery. I replied facetiously that there had to be some compensation for having sex only two weeks out of the year. In fact, my comment might have contained a grain of truth; according to some, the copulatory tie could be an important part of the psychological bond that unites mates for life.

As Freya and her mate struggled and spun toward shore, their awkward physical union seemed singularly unsuited to the production of a stable psychological one, but I reminded myself not to anthropomorphize, the gasps and writhings of human intercourse might probably seem similarly unpleasant to a wolf.

I had no idea what we would do if someone went after the wolves. I could have asked Sam to land between the humans and the wolves, but whether he would have been willing to risk one of his planes I'll never know, for fortunately the wolves reached the shore and disappeared among the trees without interference.

The frequency of raised-leg urinations by both Freya and her mate in the days preceding their tie suggested that scent marking might play an important role in courtship as well as in territoriality. Clearly I needed to see some scent marking up close if I were ever to understand this role, but so far Red and Gray, though sexually mature, had been totally uncooperative. I mentioned this problem in one of my nightly telephone reports to Hunt. His observations of captive wolves suggested that a receptive female might encourage Red and Gray to raise their legs. He said he'd see what he could do about getting a female.

He was better than his word. Within a week, two females were delivered to the wolf enclosure. They were wolf-dog hybrids, not pure wolves, but both were showing blood, a sure sign of estrus, when they were placed in the pen adjacent to Red and Gray's, and their effort could not have been more dramatic. The morning after the females arrived, every tree in the males' pen was crusted with yellow rime. A double furrow had been worn into the hard-packed snow along the fence separating the males from the females. Red and one of the females were pacing side by side, turning together as they reached each corner. For once Red ignored me, continuing his tango with the female as I took my usual place, recorded the locations of the scent marks, and shot a few feet of movie film. Gray lay in the corner, his eyes following the pacing pair and occasionally fixing on the other female, striding nervously in the far corner.

After a few minutes Red interrupted his pacing to raise a leg against a tree in the center of the pen. Gray added his mark immediately. I was ecstatic; I had finally seen wolves scent mark at close range. I spent the day filling page after page with descriptions of facial expressions, ear and tail positions, and vocalizations associated with each one of the RLUs that Red and Gray courteously provided.

At dusk, I drove back to the lab, scheming. I would first have to make sure that it was the females, not the lengthening day or some other confounding factor, that caused the scent marking. This I could do easily by removing the females for a few days to see what happened to RLU rates. If they fell and then rose again when the females were reintroduced, I could be fairly sure that the females were responsible. Then I could begin to see how the effect was communicated, maybe by removing the females again and sprinkling a little of their urine around . . . I was sufficiently absorbed in these schemes to drive right past the entrance to the lab. I turned around at Birch Road, had a quick supper, and fell asleep over my notes.

The wolves, as usual, had schemes of their own. When I arrived the next day, I could hear a pandemonium of barks, yips, and whimpers even before I cut the motor. I ran to the enclosure. Red had somehow grabbed one of the females through the fence. As he held her by the scruff of her neck, Gray lunged again and again, smashing the fence into her as he tried to get a mouthful of her flank. I grabbed the hammer that hung on the fence, dived through the gate, and locked it behind me. Spreading my parka wide and screaming at the top of my lungs, I rushed toward Red and Gray. Gray ran immediately to the far end of the pen and stood watching. Red flopped onto his back, tucked his forelegs onto his chest, and peed onto his belly. I stuck the hammer in my belt and scratched him behind the ears until he rolled onto his feet and tried to lick my face. Keeping one eye on Gray, I pushed Red away and backed out of the gate.

The female had a couple of nasty gashes, but they weren't bleeding much, so I decided not to risk administering first aid. I phoned the females' owner, who said she'd come by later that day to take them home.

On my next visit to Red and Gray, there was no more scent marking, so it probably had been the females that had revved them up; I would need another female if I were to see any more RLUs.

Hunt called that night. When I related the week's events, he agreed that it would be worthwhile to introduce another female. An hour later he called back to say he'd made arrangements with the Canadian Wildlife Service to have a female wolf delivered to the airport at Thunder Bay, at the north end of Lake Superior. When I expressed some doubts about getting a wolf through U.S. customs, he replied that the wolf would come with all the permits and certificates I'd need—and if there were any problems, he was sure I would think of something. He rang off, leaving me wondering what the penalty was for wolf smuggling.

The Thunder Bay airport was a tower, two hangars, and a terminal, the latter nearly buried in snow. I followed a plow out onto the Tarmac and waited behind the wheel as a dark green crate was unloaded from a battered de Havilland. The crate was large enough to make me worry that it might not fit into the travelall. I probably couldn't handle the wolf without drugs, but with them I'd never get through customs, so I had left them at the lab. With a little jockeying, though, the crate did fit.

Once it was safely stowed, I took a closer look at my cargo. Two rows of fifty-caliber holes went around the sides of the crate. Putting an eye to a hole, I could just discern a dark form huddled motionless in a corner. I placed an ear over a hole near the wolf to listen for breathing and got the tip of her warm, moist tongue for my trouble.

She'd probably been without water all morning, so I pulled over to the nearest snowbank and stuffed snow through the holes. I could hear her get to her feet and chomp down the snow as I climbed behind the wheel.

The trip to the border was uneventful, but as we neared the U.S. customs post at Lesbos River, I could feel my pulse throbbing in my neck. Within a few minutes I was handing the inspector my sheaf of forms. He narrowed his eyes at my beard and Levi's jacket, ignored the forms, and waved me over to the inspection area, where I was coldly greeted by two guards wearing dark blue jump suits and carrying .357s. Their long-billed recon caps bore insignia that seemed for an instant to feature crossed joints and syringes, but that must have been a hallucination fostered by my mounting anxiety. I started to hand over my sheaf of forms, hoping to disarm them with its bureaucratic bulk, but one of them told me to shut up and kept a gimlet eye on me while the other popped the hood.

The search was highly educational—I would never have thought of some of the places they looked. Eventually the tailgate was dropped, and I was asked, not politely, what was in the crate. "It's a wolf," I replied. "Honest. I've got the paper work right here." I reached for the door handle.

"Freeze." The command was spoken quietly, but his hand was on his gun. I froze. "Get a crowbar, Frank," he continued. "We'll see what this sawed-off little wimp is really trying to bring in."

"Why don't you look at my forms?" I pleaded. If they opened the crate and she tried to run, they'd blow her away.

"We'll handle it" was the reply. The other narc returned with a crowbar and with one powerful yank sprang one edge of the lid free. Before he could react, the wolf had thrust her coal black head through the opening, white teeth flashing, flicked out a long red tongue, and licked his face up one side and down the other.

"Holy cow," murmured the other narc, "it is a wolf." His partner had jumped back off the tailgate, and the wolf lunged, trying to squeeze through the opening. One more try, and she'd make it. I forgot about the .357s and ran to the rear of the vehicle, jumped onto the tailgate, shoved her nose back into the crate, and slammed the lid shut.

"*Now* will you look at my forms?" I asked. The cop with the crowbar snatched the forms from my outstretched hand, conferred briefly with his partner, and disappeared with the forms into the office. He returned a few minutes later and grudgingly admitted that everything seemed to be in order.

The sky was clearing, and from the cliffs near Nematodia I tried to see Isle Royale, where L. D. Mech had conducted his study on wolves and moose. I stopped to push more snow through the wolf's air holes and to stretch my legs, wondering what would drive any animal to that distant silver of slate then invisible even from the clifftop. Black water glistened beyond the buckled pack ice that extended halfway across the lake. It was not only for the wolf's sake that I turned the heater up as soon as I climbed back behind the wheel.

In Linde there were five mangled road kills to pick up

at the ranger station. With one more wolf to feed we'd need every deer we could get. In the front window of the ranger's residence hung a beautiful gray winter wolf pelt.

It was nearly dark when I got to the enclosure, but there was still plenty to do. Hunt wanted me to put a radio collar on our new guest in case she leaped the fence, a feat he claimed was well within the power of any healthy wolf. I did not ask why Red and Gray had never done so, assuming that knowing no life but that of captivity, they would have little motive for escape. The new wolf was different. We did not know at what age she had been captured or how she would respond to unfamiliar surroundings. Besides, if I tranquilized her, I could collect some blood and anal-sac secretions for analysis, the latter of interest because of the role they might play in scent marking.

Murmuring what I hoped were words of comfort, I slid the box off the tailgate and walked it, as gently as I could, to the gate of the enclosure. As I feared, it wouldn't go through. I'd have to give her the injection outside the pen, but I wasn't particularly worried. At the customs station she had seemed fairly tame. With Red and Gray safely in the east pen, I loaded the syringe and carefully placed it, needle down, in my rear pocket. I used the hammer to pry up one edge of the lid, holding the other hand ready to push the wolf back if she tried to escape. The nails gave suddenly with a shriek, the black snout appeared again, and before I could jerk my hand away, a pink tongue began to lick it feverishly.

A jab from a syringe was hardly a fair reply to this friendly greeting but was preferable to wrestling her into the pen. I gave her the handle of the hammer to chew on, jabbed the needle into her shoulder, and pressed the pis-

88

ton. Twenty minutes later she was still trying to push her head under the lid, but less vigorously, and in half an hour I was able to remove the lid completely. Her eyes, which I could see clearly for the first time, were yellow. They were unfocused, and her movements were jerky and uncoordinated, but when I tried to pull her out, she took my cuff in her jaws and wouldn't let go, so I gave her another half dose.

An hour after the first injection she was conscious but limp. With my arms under her forelegs and her back hugged to my chest I was able to lift her out of the crate and half drag, half carry her into the pen. After securing the gate behind us, I weighed her. I was surprised to find that she weighed only fifty pounds, half the weight of either Red or Gray.

I had prepared a radio collar while I waited for the drugs to take effect, but getting it on her was a problem. She seemed to understand what I was up to and wanted no part of it, for when I sat still, she would career over, fall onto her side, and roll onto her back, tongue lolling and legs spread so that her hips formed a lyre, but when I reached for the collar, she staggered drunkenly away. Even tranquilized, she could easily evade my tackles. Three times she hopped nimbly to the side to watch me slide on my chest through a mixture of snow, mud, and wolf shit.

I never did get the collar on her. When I'd had my fill of horse-play, I sat against the fence, puzzled by her resistance to the drugs. The two doses should have immobilized her, but she was still on her feet, sniffing at the ground, pointedly ignoring Red, who sat gaping at the fence separating the two pens. Eventually she wove her way over to him, almost colliding with a tree along the way. She sniffed his face, he growled softly, and she returned to her investigation of the pen, from time to time veering from her uncertain course to rub her flank against my knee or pluck playfully at my soiled jacket.

When I was sure the drugs had worn off to the point where there was no danger of convulsion, I left the pen to the accompaniment of piteous whines and yelps from the new captive. They followed me all the way to the truck, and when I stopped at the top of the hill and rolled down the window to listen, I could still hear them. The new wolf's yelps were backed by throaty moans I recognized as Red's. Gray, too, began to howl. With all three howling, the chorus echoed off the trees. It sounded as though half the wolves in the north were out there trying to scare the banshees.

To my relief the female was still there when I returned at dawn. She whined as I entered the pen, threw herself at my feet, rolled over, and peed on herself. There was a little blood on her swollen vulva, which meant she might still be in heat. This was a pleasant surprise, for the breeding season was officially over. Whatever the other females had that stimulated RLUs in the males, though, the new one didn't have it. As I walked up to her pen, Red urinated from a squat.

It may have been my imagination, but there seemed to be an accusation in his gaze, so I changed course and entered his pen instead. As usual, I sat down near the gate to let him make the initial approach. He padded cautiously over to me and licked my face. I scratched him behind the ears until he went for a bootlace. Foiled when I tucked my feet beneath me, he got a mouthful of beard. I grabbed his snout, squeezed the corners of his mouth to make him let go, and leaped to my feet. He pulled out of my grasp and began to nip at the already tattered cuffs of my venerable leather jacket. I pushed him away, but as far as he was concerned, this was only an invitation to further tomfoolery. He circled, jumped me from behind, and with two quick nips consumed the back of my collar. I whirled, opening the front of the jacket and exposing the fragrant red lining, which he ripped completely out with one quick tug. By the time I slipped through the gate, both sleeves were shredded to the elbow, and the collar hung by a thread. Gray lay in a corner, contentedly munching my hat.

By early afternoon Red and the female had struck up a kind of acquaintance. Though separated by the fence, they snarled and growled at each other, and for an instant Red had one of her ears between his teeth. She jerked free, yelping loudly, but the contrast between her intact ear and my ruined jacket convinced me that Red's intentions were not entirely malicious.

As though to confirm my opinion, she was back at the fence in an instant, rubbing her flanks against it until it creaked. Red sniffed her rear with no sign of aggression. Throughout the rest of the afternoon their snarls and growls grew softer, the intervals between them longer. Once they even touched noses, a sure sign of growing amity. A few minutes later the female presented her rear with her tail held brazenly to the side. Red thrust his nose through the fence, sniffing, licking, and salivating copiously. He kept his ears and tail down, humble as an anxious suitor. The female's posture was appropriately haughty; she fixed her gaze on a distant horizon, held her ears and tail erect, and endured his attention like a lady allowing a commoner to kiss her foot.

Encouraged by these signs of sexual interest, I decided

to let Red into her pen. If she were by some miracle still in heat, it would not be for long. Just in case there was trouble, I went to get Joe Lijokki, who cared for the wolves and lived nearby. Even if there were no fight, he would want to see what happened when Red met his first full-blooded female wolf. A few minutes later, we stood silently at the fence, watching for signs of lingering aggression for a few minutes, and then Joe asked if I'd named the female. I said I hadn't.

"You could do like Doc Hunt," he said with a one-sided smile, "and give her a number."

"Yeah, or I could call her Black, to go with Red and Gray."

Joe hunkered, and I followed suit. The silence grew as we watched Red and the female pacing together. There was a name hovering tantalizingly just beyond awareness, a name of someone I had never met yet somehow seemed to know, someone whose seductiveness, like the wolf's, was not of appearance but of style. Then the name came like a long-awaited sneeze. "Lotte," I said, "let's call her Lotte."

Joe grunted as he rose, in assent or effort I couldn't tell. Tucking the hammer under his belt, he entered the pen and opened the connecting gate. Ears and tail down, Red trotted into Lotte's pen. Joe locked the gate behind him, ducked through the entrance, and locked it as well. Red ignored Lotte in favor of the urine she'd sprinkled around the perimeter until she ran up to sniff his face. He growled fiercely, but she stood her ground. Then he slammed her to the ground with a swing of his hips, and she went for his throat. They began to fight furiously, with hideous growls and yelps. Although Red's advantage in size was partially balanced by Lotte's greater speed and agility, it was by no means an even match. Red knocked her over with a single blow from a forepaw, grabbed her nape, and began to shake her from side to side, but just as Joe and I were about to break it up, he relented. To our amazement Lotte immediately came back for more. This time Red ignored the sniffs delivered to his rear and snarled only when she sniffed his face. When she mounted him from the rear, however, the fight resumed. Once again Red, though clearly the victor, gave up first, and once again both wolves were unscathed.

Three more times Lotte importuned him until he attacked. Each time he tolerated her harassment a little longer, and each time his reprisal was milder. Eventually her approach aroused only a slight lip curl and a low growl, and for the rest of the afternoon he bore her attentions stoically, even when she again mounted him from the rear, clasped his waist with her forepaws, and gave him a series of vigorous pelvic thrusts.

At sunset Joe left for the warmth of the house, leaving me to watch the wolves from the truck. Like a great red footlight, the sinking sun threw the wolves' antic shadows across the snow, bathing their unschooled moves in barbaric splendor. They sniffed and licked, snarled and snapped, blundering ineluctably through a labyrinth of gestures and replies, groping for a climax.

I felt I was seeing what was not meant to be seen, a strange sentiment for a scientist, but at least I was not the only voyeur. Gray lay in the other pen, chin on the ground between his paws. I put the 10 x 50s on him and watched his amber eyes follow the dance. Then he found the dark disks of my lenses and stared directly into them. In the abstract intimacy of the powerful binoculars his eyes were cold, pale, and unblinking. It is no wonder that the ancient

Greeks believed that the gaze of a wolf could strike one dumb.

In the deepening dusk, colors vanished one by one. The wolves assumed in the dimness the artless grace of erotic ritual. Nothing was suggested; every gesture was its own meaning. Lotte passed under Red's nose, her tail languidly brushing his cheek. He pranced around to stand before her, ears and tail held high. The wolves froze, baring their teeth, arching their necks, tails wafting slowly to the side, then lashing quickly back. They seemed inflated with fury as their fur stood on end. Then they exploded into a dark, whirling chaos: flashing teeth, whipping tails, paws scratching for purchase on the frozen snow, growls, yelps, and then a gasping wheeze as Lotte was hurled into the fence.

The fight was over as suddenly as it had begun. Red strutted, and Lotte minced, then leaped to the roof of the doghouse, where she stood while Red reared onto his hind legs to touch her nose with his. Their breaths hissed, plumed, and vanished in the dark air.

When it got too dark to see, I drove back to the lab, the heater blowing delicious warmth across my quivering legs.

I arrived at Joe's the next morning with high hopes of a Lotte transformed by love. It was obvious, however, that nothing had changed. She continued to tease Red but would not stand for his inept attempts to mount. His closest approach to copulation was a mount from the rear, complete with pelvic thrusts, but with his penis about a foot from Lotte's vagina.

For the rest of the week there was no more snarling and growling. In their place appeared nose touching, anal sniffing, and "standing over," a display ordinarily interpreted as an attempt to establish dominance, in which one wolf places its forelegs over another's back from the side. Unfortunately for those who look to wolves for parallels to Western sex roles, it was Lotte, not Red, who displayed this behavior. She established her liberation in other ways, including raising her leg to urinate, which is also considered a sign of dominance; Red, as though accepting her claim, continued to squat.

At least once a day I wrestled with them both. During each match I tried to check Lotte's vulva without arousing Red's indignation. It was no longer swollen and no longer stained with blood. I had to admit that there would be no pups this year. Wolves, unlike dogs, require a lengthy and elaborate courtship. There would be a much better chance next year, so I should not have been disappointed, but I was.

Since Red had tolerated my inspection of Lotte's genitals, it was probably safe to open the gate to Gray's pen to give all three wolves access to both pens and to each other. When I did so, the wolves exchanged pens and frantically checked all the odors. Then Lotte went after Gray and pursued him in a ten-minute flat-out chase around the perimeters of both pens. Twice Lotte tried to stand over him, but each time he pinned her throat to the ground, and on her third approach a slight curl of his lip sent her into the other pen.

Thus, in matters of rank as in all others, Gray remained an enigma. He would not compete with Red, not even for Lotte. Nor would he go for a juicy deer leg that I threw over the fence in his general direction. Instead, he shied away, leaving it to Lotte and Red, who began a tug-of-war. On the other hand, Red and Lotte often surrendered to Gray the warm patches of morning sunlight in which they all loved to bask. To complicate matters further, Red monopolized any food placed in the enclosure unless it was divided and placed in widely separated locations so he could not guard it all, but when I threw in a large rubber ball, it was Lotte who pounced on it, and she was able to repulse Red's attempts to take it from her. Both Red and Lotte competed for scratches from any human who came to the fence. When Lotte attempted to get between Red and the potential masseur, Red snapped at her, and though he missed by at least an inch, she yelped so convincingly that he jumped back, and as usual she was the one who got the massage. As an apprentice ethologist I felt I ought to be able to assign each wolf a rank, but the better I got to know them, the harder that was to do.

With no more courtship to watch, I returned to tracking. The days were longer, consequently, so were my samples of tracks, but there was a price to pay. With rising temperatures and a week or more between snowfalls, I was often snowshoeing through dirty slush, the wolf tracks barely visible among the leaves and other detritus uncovered by the thaw. Some bare patches on south-facing slopes were certain to have received scent marks that I could not see, so on hands and knees I sniffed every likely stump and from time to time was rewarded with the acrid, musky odors of wolf urine. My snowshoes became instruments of torture, gathering five-pound clumps of snow that had to be endured or kicked off at every step. As a final frustration, even on fresh snow the rate of scent marking had dropped drastically from its peak during the breeding season, so I was deprived of the minor satisfaction of seeing the number of RLUs I'd recorded grow steadily day by day.

The sun no longer lay reliably in the southern sky; Orion clambered over the horizon earlier every day. Spring was marching north at double time, and winter was beating a hasty retreat. The lakes got slushy and the planes shed their skis. Until the ice cleared and we could use floats, we would take off and land on wheels at Axe International. I would do no more tracking on remote frozen lakes until next winter.

The stack of wolf carcasses behind the garage would soon begin to thaw, but I wanted to keep the anal sacs frozen, for Hunt suggested that they might be involved in scent marking and we had decided to analyze their contents. Rather than excavate the sacs themselves, I used a crosscut saw to remove the posteriors of five carcasses, packed them in a box labeled "Wolf Recta" and stashed the box in the lab's enormous freezer.

Hunt called one evening to ask if I'd be willing to deliver a progress report at the American Institute of Biological Sciences (AIBS) meeting in Northton. I agreed with enthusiasm, for the change of season had brought my work to a point of diminishing returns and Northton was more or less on one way back to Ann Arbor, where there were instruments to analyze anal sacs and computers to digest my data.

6

Wolf Woods

Yellow and lime leaflets played peekaboo in sunlit tree-tops, Labrador tea flourished in the receding snow, and even the lichen seemed alive. On north-facing slopes, though, the snow was still knee-deep; old-timers claimed they could find enough to make ice cream on the Fourth of July.

The morning was cold enough to make me sprint back to the lodge after dumping each load in my trunk, cold enough, I hoped, to keep the wolf recta frozen until I got to Northton, where I would pack them in dry ice before I joined Hunt at the meetings. I stowed them in the corner, where they would do the least damage if they thawed, then zoomed at Hunt-like speeds to Joe's for a farewell romp with the wolves.

As I strode to the fence, Red and Lotte arched and leaped, gamboling so frantically that even Gray had to dance a little, if only to keep out of their way. I made my escape after only the briefest of romps, backing through the gate like a mandarin, pushing them back as they tried to squeeze past.

I howled from the top of the hill. They replied immediately, Lotte barking and yipping, Red croaking like a raven, and only Gray sounding like a wolf. At Upsala Lake I stopped for a howl to Freya, who did not reply.

I made it to Northton in record time. I met Hunt at the University of Northland, where the AIBS meetings were already in progress. My talk went well, in spite of my nervousness. Afterward I went home with Hunt for dinner.

Over dinner Hunt, his family, and I discussed such a variety of topics that wolves were conspicuous by their absence. At its closest approach to that topic the conversation was curiously becalmed. We were discussing Breezy, the dog, a small terrierlike creature of the sort that is ordinarily found in orbit about one's feet, preparing to muffle its yips with a mouthful of ankle. Unlike others of his ilk, however, Breezy, perhaps because of his advancing age, was calm, almost reserved. In an inept attempt to compliment the Hunts on their dog's disposition, I remarked that his size and personality must make him much easier to live with than Hurricane, their wolf, had been.

Hunt and Charlotte exchanged glances. Even the children fell momentarily silent. Suddenly there were dishes to clear, homework assignments to be done, a bed to be made. When we all had retired, I pulled from my pack my well-thumbed copy of Hunt's book and reread the apology with which he had ended his epilogue. I fell asleep with the book on my chest, wondering where Hurricane was now.

I rose with the Hunt family, said a quick farewell, and left for Chicago. By late afternoon, I was on the Kennedy

Expressway, threading my way through impending grid-
lock on my way to an appointment with Daniel Baer at
the Chicago Zoo. Baer is a dour, contained man with a
wit like water in the desert: seldom near the surface and
quicksand when it is. He asked me to describe what kinds
of data I hoped to gather at Wolf Woods, as the zoo's wolf
exhibit was called. I replied that I was after any variable
that might relate to frequency of scent marking, including
season, sex, rank, and mood. In his slow, flat basso he
pointed out that seasonal data would require observations
over a period of at least a year. How often, he asked, did
I plan to come to the zoo?

I'd have to see, I answered, but I thought once a month
would probably be enough. He suggested that dawn, dusk,
and feeding time would be the best times to observe since
all activities, including scent marking, are more frequent
at those times. Observations at dawn and dusk, when the
zoo was closed to the public, would require a key. He
rose, led me downstairs to the security office, and issued
me one. As I left, I had to force myself not to skip and
giggle, for I clutched warmly in my hand a fantasy enter-
tained since my first visit to the Chicago Zoo at the age
of eight: a master key to the zoo.

I used my key at dawn and walked unchallenged through
the deserted zoo to Wolf Woods. If Lotte and Red had
performed a pas de deux, the Chicago Zoo wolves were
the Bolshoi, complete with prima ballerinas, a corps de
ballet, and even an audience. A pure white wolf stood
atop a large, bare mound, surveying the antics of six others
cavorting around it. By the time I reached the fence, I'd
seen more hip slams, hackle raisings, snarls, and chases
than I would in an entire day at our enclosure in the north.
So far I'd seen only seven of the nine wolves, but used

as I was to watching only three, they were a horde, a milling mass of indistinguishable animals. How would I ever learn to tell them apart? Learning to identify individuals is the first task of any ethologist conducting a long-term study of a group. In the confusion of that first morning that task seemed impossible.

I had just begun a list of features that I hoped would help me recognize some of the wolves when a diminutive woman with close-cropped ashen hair rode up in an electric golf cart. Her dark-haired female driver produced a stenographic notebook and scribbled frantically as the passenger began calling out pairs of numbers linked by prepositions: "Female Four to Two; Two to Four. Female Six over Male Five. Male Seven to Female Four. Male Seven down." I tried to connect the code to the behavior of the wolves but could not; it was all going much too fast. "Keeper in," said the small woman. That I could understand. A young woman with a heavy bucket had just entered. The wolves formed a line on the mound with military precision. The keeper threw one piece of meat after another, and as each piece sailed through the air, a wolf ran to catch it. Only twice did two lunge simultaneously; each time the woman dictated another pair of numbers. Each wolf took its piece of meat and ran off to consume it away from the others.

Seeing my notebook, the driver asked if I was Peters. Without waiting for a reply, she introduced her companion as Lisa Baer, wife of Daniel. For the next half hour Lisa ran through a crash course in identifying the wolves, gave me a brief history of the pack, and then zoomed off to check her ground squirrel traps, explaining, even as the cart began to move, that she was tagging them in order to map their territories.

In the course of my four-day visit to the zoo I learned that I had just seen Lisa Baer at her slowest speed. Ordinarily she was a blur, appearing at the zoo library, which she was reorganizing; the bookstore, which she managed; the zoo hospital, where she assisted; and, of course, at Wolf Woods, where, with or without her colleague, she gathered more data in twenty minutes than I could manage to get down in an entire day.

Her assistance was invaluable in my continuing attempts to identify the wolves. She pointed out Male Five's dark mask and Male Six's crooked tail, the dark hip patch and rough mane that distinguished Female Seven from Female Eight. She was also able to explain why my counts of the wolves kept coming up short: One wolf, Male Two, rarely left the den.

Male Two, Lisa explained, was the patriarch. Even in captivity wolves are very old at ten. Male Two was sixteen. Crippled by arthritis, he left the den only on the warmest of afternoons, ordinarily remaining inside at mealtime, when another wolf would bring him food. "Watch Female Seven," Lisa advised. "She's been feeding him lately." Sure enough, the next day Female Seven disappeared into the den with a hunk of meat and emerged a few seconds later without it. That afternoon was clear and warm. With temperatures in the fifties, Male Two made an appearance. He was immediately mobbed by the rest of the wolves. They leaped over each other as they tried to lick his face. The melee quickly became a group ceremony that climaxed in a howl. Male Two stood quietly amid the chaos. When the howl subsided, he painfully crept back into the den.

Lisa and Daniel Baer were, like Hunt, victims of the economics of data reduction. Lisa gathered data at feeding time nearly every day, and Daniel spent two weeks during every breeding season taking notes whenever there was enough light to see. Confronted with a choice between gathering new data and analyzing the data they already had, they generally chose the former, for analysis could always be postponed, while the new developments in the relations among the wolves could not. The result was a closetful of notes, only the most interesting ten percent of which ever saw the light of day.

I owed the Baers far more than the data I collected: dawn walks through the deserted zoo; exotic birds shrieking brightly against the low roar of distant traffic; a distant siren and an answering howl. Every morning, as they frolicked in the cold morning air, the wolves revealed new complexities in their dance. I began to realize that any wolf's change of position, posture, or expression affected every other wolf in the enclosure. When Female Six moved to follow a patch of warm sunlight that crept across the rear of the pen, Female Four, the matriarch, watching from her commanding position atop the mound, shifted her position so that Female Six remained under her gaze. Female Five, ambling toward the pond, veered sharply to avoid that gaze, her detour taking her past Male Six, who backed up to avoid her, colliding with Male Seven, who snarled defensively. His snarl drew a low growl from Female Four, as a result of which two other wolves on the mound got up and moved away, displacing Female Six from her patch of sunlight.

The German ethologist Schenkel wrote that every relationship in a pack concerns every member. At Wolf Woods it was easy to see his point. The mechanics of movement were not Newtonian, but they were orderly nonetheless, a calculus of attraction and repulsion, coalition and autonomy, which united the pack in a web of resonating sensitivities.

Half an hour before feeding time on my fourth and last day a young female trotted over to another young wolf and touched his nose with hers. Receiving no response, she raised a forepaw and gently batted at the lying wolf, who rolled over, gaping. The female grabbed his snout. The two jaw-wrestled for a few seconds until the second wolf leaped to his feet and with a bouncy, rocking gait ran behind the mound, the young female snapping at his heels. As soon as she disappeared behind the mound, there was a cartoonlike explosion of barks and yips, and not two but five wolves flew over the top of the mound to stand, panting, by the pond. Female Four trotted around the mound; the young wolves ran to greet her. They crowded around, each using hip slams and sinuous wriggles to interpose itself between Female Four and the others. Female Four stood regally, with head and tail high, suffering their enthusiasm with great dignity. The older wolves, scattered in various shady nooks about the enclosure, now began to appear, stretching like joggers before a run, then converging on the melee. Soon seven wolves were milling and leaping at Female Four. One of the younger wolves was ejected from the writhing mass. He walked a few yards away, raised his head, and emitted a series of high yips, a pitiful imitation of a howl.

Unpracticed as his performance was, its effect was immediate. Two other wolves left the tumble, sat, and began to howl. Soon all eight wolves were howling in an atonal chorus that built and echoed. It was a Schönberg concerto with cadenzas by Coltrane. When it ended, the wolves began to disperse.

As the howl faded into the trees, a small crowd of people began to gather, shouting inanities at the wolves and shrieking at them to get them to howl again—but when a howling session is over, as this one was, wolves enter a fifteen-minute refractory period during which nothing in the world can get them to howl again. Some speculate that the function of the refractory period is to allow all the packs in an area to hear each other. By remaining silent after a howl and listening for replies, a pack can learn where other packs in the vicinity are.

Among the last to join the crowd at the fence was an eight-year-old boy whose cunning little outfit had, I was sure, graced the pages of a recent issue of the New Yorker. He turned to his father and, pointing to the sign identifying the wolves, piped, "Look, Daddy, wolves."

The father replied, "No, Kent, those aren't wolves. Wolves don't look like dogs—they're big and mean."

Daddy dragged Kent off just as Female Four moved slowly to the top of the mound, her retinue in procession behind her. The wolves lined up on the mound forming a perfect row, all staring at the gate. It was feeding time. Lisa Baer glided up in her golf cart, said a quick hello, and began to scribble. Male Four trotted to the gate as the keeper arrived and followed her to the area in front of the mound. She threw chunks of turkey to the wolves on the mound, then handed the last chunk to Male Four, who kept it between his jaws as he escorted her to the gate. He ate half, then carried the other half to the den, disappeared inside, and reappeared two seconds later without it. For a moment I imagined the old wolf lying in the den, watching shadows on the wall, blinded by the light whenever he looked outside.

Soon all the wolves were lying in the sun, oblivious to the howls, catcalls, and insults of the visitors. The show was over.

Perhaps it was only because I didn't know the wolves

well enough, but it seemed that dominance was much more important at the Chicago Zoo than at Joe's. It was the dominant pair that escorted the keeper in and out at mealtime and that produced most of the scent marks I saw. The power of rank was dramatically illustrated on that last afternoon, when Female Four froze a large young male in his tracks merely by raising her head off her paws and glancing in his direction. He was more than fifteen yards away, but he put his tail down, his ears back, and skulked away to sulk behind a bush.

As clouds piled up in the west, the wolves flopped down one by one, needing only brandy and cigars to complete the image of postprandial contentment. When the rain began, they paid it no attention, snoozing on as chilly rivulets ran off their backs. I was not so well protected, and my notes began to turn to paste. It was time to get back to Ann Arbor. I gathered my gear and squished off to my vehicle. I turned to wave, but the wolves ignored me. To them I was just another nameless visitor.

The author at work. (*Bonnie Clements.*)

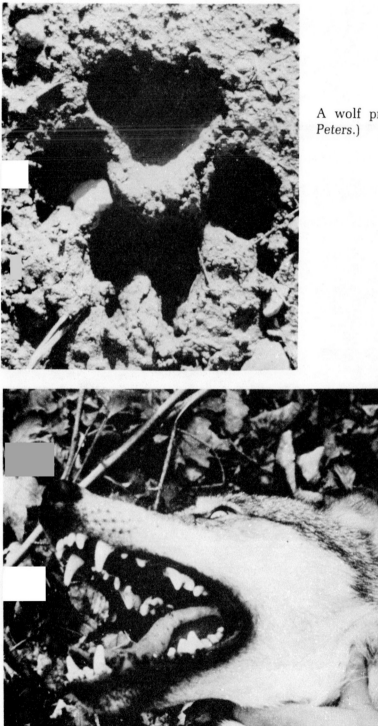

A wolf print. (Roger Peters.)

A wolf's tools for survival. (Roger Peters.)

Gray paces uneasily. (*Roger Peters.*)

Passive submission at the zoo. (*Roger Peters.*)

Threat. (*Roger Peters.*)

A group howl. (*Roger Peters.*)

Courtship bow by Red. (*Roger Peters.*)

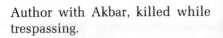

Author with Akbar, killed while trespassing.

Lotte and Red touch noses during early courtship. (*Roger Peters.*)

7

Independent Variables

Ann Arbor in the spring: pastel dresses blooming on rain-darkened sidewalks; soft pink petals fluttering on black branches; lime green leaflets against a gunmetal sky. Every morning there were deer in the arboretum, munching last winter's windfalls and staring at human intruders with the insouciance of gum-chewing hoods. Barn swallows were back, strafing anyone who ventured near the stadium. All along the Huron River the amphibian philharmonic opened the season with an invention by Varèse, peepers peeping, chorus frogs croaking, bullfrogs bumping pizzicato on bass.

Through this vernal celebration I slouched like a troll. Far away in the north Freya was digging her den, but this was cause for concern, not for joy. With the deer population at its lowest in decades, it was no time to be having pups. I could not have done anything for her even if I were at Ontolagon; nevertheless, I wished I were there.

Instead, I was in Ann Arbor, busy every night analyzing the contents of the frozen anal sacs I had sawed from frozen wolves the week before.

A less romantic avenue to the mind of the wolf would be hard to imagine. Anal sacs are grape-sized pouches that open into the recta of wolves, dogs, and many other carnivores. Their position virtually ensures that their secretions will coat the surface of large firm feces. Their pungent odor is powerful; it is mainly the odor of anal sacs that wolves and dogs savor when they sniff each others' scats or rears. Since anal-sac secretions might act as scent marks, I hoped to learn what, if anything, their odors meant. My interest in mental maps had led me from one end of the wolf to the other.

I had already found a chromatograph, a device for analyzing complex mixtures into component compounds. I'd be allowed to use it when the chemists didn't need it— at night. I was able to run three samples my first night and four the second. The results were encouraging. The relative proportions of short-chain fatty acids varied dramatically from wolf to wolf. I had more than one anal sac sample from only one wolf, Red, and those had been collected only a month apart, but they were remarkably similar. Anal scent might, therefore, be a kind of olfactory signature, an announcement of a wolf's identity. It was too soon to run from the lab shouting, "Eureka," though, for what mattered was not whether a machine could recognize characteristic combinations of components but whether wolves do. Work on that question would have to wait.

After a month of nightly vigils at the gas chromatograph I was ready to return to Ontolagon. Early in June I was on my way.

Independent Variables

Journeys are like the trompes l'oeil in which a rabbit suddenly becomes a duck, a vase a face, or a rat a man. On a journey, "from" can become "to" with similar abruptness. On my excursions to the north the change came with the first intimations of the lake. Long before it came into view, I knew Superior was there. Perhaps it was the birches that began in the headwaters of the Escanaba, or the lay of the land, rolling yet sloping generally down, or the resulting enthusiasm in the engine. Whatever the cue, somewhere in northern Michigan my journey was no longer away from home but toward Freya, Lotte, and the forest.

There were deer browsing along the edge of the road a couple of miles north of Marquette. They didn't even look up as I rushed by. I tried to view them as a wolf would, but I could not see them as venison or arouse a trace of lust for their blood. Another attempt at naked wolfery was equally unsuccessful: I howled from the highway as I entered the national forest, but the only reply was a woody echo.

The next stop was Joe's. The VW was gone, and the house dark, so Joe had probably taken his family into Axe to see a movie. Red and Lotte pranced in my headlights. Gray paced back and forth behind them.

I cut the lights and walked to the pen in the dark. At the sound of my voice Red hurled himself against the fence, ears pinned back, whining for a scratch. He whimpered frantically as I stroked his flank, as though the pleasure were too much to bear. The whimpers turned to growls at Lotte's approach. She scuttled away, only to circle and approach from behind. For a moment I was able to scratch one wolf with each hand. Then Red, sensing that his pleasure had been reduced by half, whirled and snapped. Although his jaws missed her by half a yard, Lotte yelped and limped away, favoring an uninjured paw.

I tossed them some bones, putting several in each corner so Gray could get some once he had assured himself they were safe. I left to the sounds of happy crunching, punctuated by low growls as one of them, probably Lotte, tried to diversify his or her portfolio.

At the lab I was greeted by Milo, who showed me Freya's den on a topo map and said he'd seen a pup on his flight that morning. We celebrated by breaking open the case of Buckhorn I'd stored in the cellar in April. "Amy and her mate had pups," Milo said.

"Maybe that'll keep her out of town for a while," I replied.

"A new pair of wolves has moved into the area just east of Beach Lake. There's a small zone unoccupied by wolves over there, between Freya's territory and the outskirts of Axe. Hunt will be up early the next week, and Bert will be back any day."

After twelve hours on the road I was poleaxed by a couple of beers and barely made it to bed.

The aroma of perking coffee wakened me. As I sat up, I noted with pleasure that I was already dressed. Tactfully avoiding any reference to the probable state of my stomach, Milo volunteered to do the flying that morning.

I was glad to defer flying for a day or two. I wanted to get started on a device with which I hoped to determine whether or not Red, Lotte, and Gray could discriminate anal scents of different wolves. I spent the morning sawing and hammering. By noon I had a bizarre contraption of plywood and two-by-fours, which I hoped would function as a kind of Skinner box for wolves.

For thirty years psychologists had used Skinner boxes to explore the sensory and intellectual capacities of pigeons and rats. A Skinner box is a small cage containing a bar or other implement that, when pressed, instantly delivers a reward, usually food. If a hungry animal can learn to press the bar in the presence of one stimulus and to refrain from pressing it in the presence of another, everything else remaining the same, the animal must be able to distinguish the two stimuli, which in my experiment would be anal-sac secretions from male and female wolves.

My Skinner box—not a box at all, for the wolves were already enclosed—had three parts. First, a long horizontal channel pivoted near its center so that when one end was pressed, it would tilt, allowing kibbled dog food to roll down to the wolf; the channel would protrude through the fence into the enclosure. Secondly, a wooden rod held a Styrofoam cup containing an anal-scent-saturated cotton ball; the rod was adjustable so the cup could be held on the side of the fence away from the wolf but close enough so that the animal could smell its contents. Finally, a large sheet of plywood cut into an irregular shape was attached to the front of my creation, with the bar protruding through it. When the machine was in position, the plywood sheet would be pressed against the fence and secured to it. It would present a distinctive signal that the game was under way and conceal from the wolves the condition, loaded or empty, of the channel. Anticipating future modifications of the prototype, I used a label maker to create a suitable insignia: "Wolf Operant Learning Feeder (WOLF), Mark I."

The next step was to get the wolves hungry enough to want the food. I balked at this initially but managed to convince myself that, since wild wolves often went a week or more without food, it would do our captive ones no harm to miss a day. Furthermore, it was Hunt's opinion

111

that Red was somewhat overweight. He would be my first subject. I drove to Joe's, got Red into the west pen and Lotte and Gray into the east pen and locked the gate connecting them. I explained to Joe what I was up to and asked him not to feed Red that night. He agreed, but only after I had explained that once Red had learned to press the bar, he'd be getting his usual amount of food—he'd just have to work for it.

The following morning I hauled the Mark I to the enclosure for the first stage of conditioning, called magazine training, in which Red would learn that pressing the bar earned him food. At first the Mark I's unusual shape was threatening, and Red paced nervously as I pushed it up to the fence. I secured it to the mesh and loaded the bar with food. As soon as he looked directly at the machine, I tripped the bar, sending five chunks of kibble rattling down the channel. As he approached to get the food, his ears pinned back and his tail curled tight under his belly, I sent another five chunks of food rolling down the channel. He grabbed a mouthful and ran to the other side of the pen, where he crunched the dog food down, never taking his eyes from the Mark I.

After a few seconds he sat watching the machine intently. When he shifted his position, coming marginally closer, I tripped the bar, and he padded over to take the food. This time he did not withdraw quite so far to eat. We repeated these maneuvers five times in the next ten minutes, at the end of which he was no longer withdrawing at all but was standing expectantly in front of the machine, staring at the bar with his head cocked quizzically. Eventually he took a tentative step toward the machine. As he raised his paw, I tipped the channel. The sudden movement startled him, and instead of taking the food, he jumped back. It took another twenty minutes to get him back in front of the machine. This time I bided my time, and soon he began to sniff the end of the bar. I waited until he began to paw at it and tipped it gently. He caught the kibble before it hit the ground and batted at the end of the bar almost before I could reload it. He gobbled the kibble, then pawed vigorously at the bar, receiving another handful of kibble. This time he held the bar down. When no more food appeared, he began to chew at the end of the bar. I unhooked the plywood shield, moved the Mark I behind the garage, and eased the pickup back to the lab. It had been a promising beginning.

I found Bert in the basement of the lodge, leveling a soldering gun at a yard-long metal cylinder that looked somewhat like a small torpedo. He explained that he was modifying a sonabuoy, a device used by the navy to record underwater sounds. Once modified, the sonabuoys would relay wolf howls to a receiver and tape recorder at the lab. These very sonabuoys had been used by Roger Payne to make his famous recordings of the songs of the humpback whale. They were on loan from Payne, a good thing, Bert added, for they were enormously expensive. Quoting Henry James's definition of science as "the absence of prejudice combined with the presence of money," I ascended the stairs to prepare lunch.

When I dragged the Mark I to the fence the next morning, Red bounced and frisked like a puppy. I loaded the bar and pushed the machine to the fence. Before I could secure it, Red had obtained a mouthful of kibble. I let him work it a few more times, then shooed him into the other pen so I could begin magazine training with Lotte.

Psychologists' lore has it that rats are more easily trained if they are gentled beforehand. Gentling consists of handling, stroking, and otherwise accustoming the animal to manipulation by the experimenter. It was my intention to gentle Lotte before beginning, but it would be difficult to find a term less appropriate for what ensued. She began sweetly enough, once again demonstrating her uncanny ability to sniff out the most minute cut or abrasion. As I sat in the dust, she pulled up my cuff, yanked down my sock, and began to tongue a small scratch I'd received during the construction of the Mark I. I scratched her gently behind the ears until she plucked at a loose boot-lace and with two quick jerks of her head undid the knot. When I pushed her away from my other boot, she darted to my belt, pulled the free end through its loop, and un-buckled it with one quick yank. I pushed her away, this time not gently, but she slid over my arm and got a mouth-ful of beard. I yelped and squeezed the corners of her mouth to make her let go, and she did, only to run her wet red tongue over both lenses of my glasses. The world became a filmy blur.

I whipped the glasses into a safe pocket and tried to rise, but as I was halfway up, Lotte lunged, knocking me flat onto my back. Straddling my chest with her forelegs, she licked my face enthusiastically. I submitted to this endearment for a moment, then rolled away and backed out the gate, glancing over my shoulder to see if Joe had seen any of this tomfoolery.

With Lotte adequately gentled, it was time to begin mag-azine training. She must have been watching as I had taught Red to press the bar, for no sooner had I moved the Mark I into position than she trotted over and pressed the lever. I quickly rolled some dog food down the chan-nel. She evidently had learned simply by observing Red. It had not even been necessary to deprive her of food. I was elated—I already had two magazine-trained subjects.

I reloaded the machine and waited for her to return for another trial. As soon as she had finished her first mouthful, which she had taken across the enclosure to devour, she padded back. This time, however, instead of pressing, she dropped to her belly, extended her head upward, and frantically licked the end of the bar. She was displaying a posture called active submission, often adopted by pups or low-ranking adults in the presence of their superiors, which often respond by regurgitating food. For pups, active submission is an important means of obtaining food and of expressing dependence.

Evidently Lotte regarded the Mark I as a sort of mechanical parent. It regurgitated food; ergo, it should respond to begging.

Whatever the logic behind Lotte's behavior, the experiment required bar pressing, not displays of submission, so I left the machine in position and let her display to her heart's content, hoping that she would learn that displaying wouldn't work. I left the machine loaded and in place while I jotted some notes on the morning's events.

Twenty minutes later Lotte lay in the corner, head on paws, mournfully gazing at the unresponsive machine. It looked as if it might take her some time to try something besides begging, so I hooked up a simple automatic reloading device, filled it with five pounds of kibble, and left.

According to Bert, the previous day a pair of wolves had walked down Beach Lake Road, which was muddy enough to take tracks. I found the tracks, three white, bony scats, and a dramatic scratch mark at a crossroad. The road surface had been gouged deeply by all four of a wolf's paws. Mud and humus had been thrown over three yards behind. It was, however, impossible to be sure that the wolves hadn't left the road at the many dry places, so the rates of sign production couldn't be compared to my winter data—they might have produced other marks off the road, where I couldn't see them.

After two hours of tracking I returned to the enclosure to find the remains of the Mark I in a heap alongside the fence. The bar and stimulus holder had disappeared, and one corner of Lotte's pen was covered with splinters of white pine. Lotte lay among them, cheerfully chewing on the tattered remains of the two-by-four that had formed the bottom of the bar. She didn't even look up. Fortunately the slapdash construction of the Mark I had allowed her to pull it apart without much damage to the rest of the machine. The automatic food hopper was not only intact but still full. She must have gone back to active submission, then attacked the machine in frustration without ever pressing the bar. In disgust I hurled the wreckage of the Mark I into the jeep. I drove back to the lab, vowing not to resume testing until I had made the WOLF completely wolfproof.

8

Howls

Bert was busy with his sonabuoys, and Milo had flown the last few times, so I did the radio tracking the next morning. The new pair of wolves that had moved into the area around Beach Lake was at the county dump, feasting on the bloated carcass of a large horse. It seemed that the men running the bulldozers and dump trucks at the other end of the landfill must see them, but Louis assured me that the piles of garbage were higher than they looked from the air and that the wolves were well out of sight. I was nevertheless tempted to violate our policy of non-intervention by asking Louis to buzz the wolves, but on our third pass they scampered for the trees on their own accord. A huge bulldozer was headed their way. The pair made it into the woods a full minute before the dozer rounded the mountain of trash.

Our next stop was Freya, whose signal again came from the den. I asked for a low pass. As the ridge whizzed by on my right, it was a blur, but with the gain turned all the way down there was one point, just below a small clearing, where Freya's signal came in clearly. There were, however, no wolves in sight.

Louis flew a spiral so I could decide which of the several logging roads in the vicinity was most likely to have tracks. As we crossed Kelly Creek, I saw a lean gray shape moving along the marshy bank. Louis had seen it, too, and he tightened our spiral. It was a wolf, moving briskly in the general direction of the den.

"Must be papa," said Louis around his cigar. "Probably bringing home the bacon."

"It must be in his belly," I replied. "There's nothing in his mouth."

The wolf hesitated several times on the bank, as though looking for a place to cross, then flung himself into the stream and half leaped, half paddled across. He flew from the water on the other side and shook himself, sending a silvery spray in all directions. He looked around as though to regain his bearings, then headed straight toward the trampled small lawn below the mouth of the den. From the air his legs were invisible; the lean gray form seemed to glide through the trees. As he neared the lawn, two tiny gray balls shot from the den and hurtled downhill toward him. They tried to leap at his face, but their momentum carried them past him as he continued without veering on his course to the den. Freya crawled out to greet him. He licked her muzzle as she struggled to her feet, then stretched his neck low as he regurgitated food at her feet. The pups bounded over to the food, but a glance from their father sent them scurrying away as Freya ate. They soon returned to harass him, however; mission accomplished, he cooperated by dropping onto his side to jaw-wrestle. They were still at it when I lowered my binoculars and pointed south toward the Olympus pack.

I was able to locate it and three other packs as well but

saw no more wolves. We returned to the seaplane base at noon. I spent the afternoon reassembling the WOLF. Bolted rather than nailed, reinforced with oblique struts at every union, and with the end of the bar sheathed in galvanized steel, it deserved a new label: "Mark II." As I manhandled it into the bed of the pickup, Hunt's station wagon glided into the parking area.

Bert was coming up the walk, a sonabuoy on his shoulder. His grimace of effort broke into a grin at the sight of Hunt. Lowering his load, he strode over to shake his hand. When the greeting was over, Hunt checked his watch and announced that even with Charlotte and the kids along he'd made the trip in just over three hours. He'd dropped the family off at a motel in Axe, he continued, stretching. They'd come along for a brief vacation and would return home to Northton with him in a few days. He then asked Bert whether he'd be out howling that evening and whether he'd mind if he, Charlotte, and the kids came along. Much of Bert's research was based on wolves' replies to his own howls, which he found both more convenient and more effective than the recordings favored by some investigators. He replied that the more people howling, the better. The Stabler Lake pack, he added, was near Muttberg Road. He planned to howl to them at dusk, when the air would be still.

While Hunt went over the flight sheets on which we'd recorded the locations of radioed wolves during the previous week, Bert and I loaded the recorder, parabolic mike, and a couple of sonabuoys into the jeep. I asked if he was merely being polite about the number of people howling. He registered dismay that I would entertain such a notion. "Of course not," he replied. "The more voices howling, the better the chances of a reply."

"Is that because more voices are louder?"

119

"Partially. But it's mainly because the pressure waves of different voices reinforce and cancel each other. Two voices howling on two different pitches produce three different tones. The third tone is a beat frequency equal to the difference between the two others."

"So three voices would produce six different pitches—one, two and three, plus one minus two, one minus three, and two minus three?"

"Right. And we'll have an extra advantage because high tones not only carry better but seem to be more stimulating. Those soprano tones from the kids and Charlotte will really help."

"Are those beat frequencies why it's so hard to tell how many wolves are howling?"

"Yeah. You can count one or two, but any more than two sound like a dozen."

After arranging a rendezvous on Mūttberg Road, Hunt left to meet his family. Over dinner I read to Bert and Milo a passage from General Grant's memoirs. Grant and his guide were traveling on horseback when they heard wolves howling a short distance ahead. The guide asked the general how many wolves he thought there were. In Grant's own words:

> Suspecting that he thought I would overestimate the number, I determined to show my acquaintance with the animal by putting the estimate below what possibly could be correct, and answered, "Oh, about twenty," very indifferently. He smiled and rode on. In a minute we were close upon them, and before they saw us. There were just *two* of them. Seated upon their haunches, with their mouths close together, they had made all the noise we had been hearing for the past ten minutes.

After dinner Bert and I piled into the jeep. As we swung past Axe, the Hunt family pulled in behind us. Twenty minutes later we approached the place where the pack had been that morning. Bert pulled over to the side of the road, and I took a bearing with a hand-held antenna. "Go up about half a mile," I suggested.

Half a mile farther along I could get the signal even before I plugged in the antenna. The radioed wolf was close. We gathered around Bert as he set up his recorder and parabolic mike. I put on earphones so I could listen to the radio signal. The beeps would become uneven in loudness if the wolf began to move.

Bert asked for silence and said he'd do the first howl alone. Starting low in the baritone range, he performed an upward glissando for about a third, then broke up an octave and slid slowly down to his original pitch. We waited for a reply, our Quaker-like silence more meditation than science. The ordinary sounds of evening were loud to our straining ears: the creaking and popping of cooling engines; a distant outboard motor; a bird's single cry; soft breathing; mosquitoes closing in. After a long three minutes Bert drew a deep breath and howled again. His echo faded from the trees, and once again we entered the evening with our ears.

The radio signal remained a monotonous stream of tiny beeps; if the wolf was moving, he was not changing elevation or going behind any large rocks. Bert cocked an eyebrow at me. "Steady," I whispered.

"Probably asleep," he suggested.

"This bunch can wake 'em up," said Hunt. "How many were with him this morning?"

"I couldn't see," I replied, "but there were four together on Monday."

"OK," said Bert. "Let's try a group howl. Everyone on a different pitch, come in at different times, and trail off gradually at the end."

It was a bloodcurdling sound. Bert kept us going with wild gyrations of his arms, then cut us off with a conductor's omega-shaped snap. Our echo had hardly faded when the wolves howled back.

Resounding through the dark woods, which suddenly seemed very close, the howl was eerie. Every malicious myth of lupine rapaciousness suddenly seemed plausible. The sound chilled my neck, ran down my back, and bristled the hair on my forearms. It made me want to run for a gun or for cover. It was a pandemonium worthy of Milton's pen, with hoots, shrieks, brays, and ululations. It built and faded, built again, then subsided into a coda of moans and yips.

The ensuing silence was not the silence after a shotgun blast or the hush after a symphony's closing chord. It was more like the silence after a scream in the night. It held a rustling procession of scarcely heard echoes, like black-hooded monks hastening past a crypt. Bert clicked off the recorder, startling us with the tiny sound. I wondered why he had recorded the silence. Would a sound spectogram of that silence show that it really was unique?

We all looked at one another, about to burst into excited chatter. Bert touched his lips. I put on the earphones. The signal had disappeared. I pantomimed walking fingers, and Bert nodded. Nylon whistled against denim as someone shifted position. The signal came back louder than before. I held the receiver so Bert could see the signal meter and the gain, now almost all the way down. He grinned.

Leaves crunched in the trees not twenty yards away.

We froze. Then, unmistakably, there was a deep "woof" from the same direction. Bert started the recorder, but it was too late. He got another five minutes of mosquitoes and distant motors, rewound, and signaled for another howl. This time we were inspired. We whooped and moaned, crying in unfelt pain, finding loneliness we hadn't known was there. Primal therapy no longer seemed so absurd. We wound down, halted, went again into meditative expectancy. Mosquitoes converged in whining clouds, but no one moved.

Five minutes passed with no reply. Then we heard a car coming down the road, its headlights flickering on the treetops.

Bert rewound once more. "If the guy in that car sees us all here, he'll stop for sure. We'll be arguing wolves and deer all night," he muttered.

"Not me," I replied. "I'm studying bullfrogs." We put the radio and recording gear into the jeep and exchanged glances, trying to decide whether or not we could get everybody into the vehicles before the interloper arrived. Suddenly Charlotte, perhaps inspired by the cabalistic atmosphere established by our hush, joined hands with two of her sons. Without a word the rest of us converged.

When the headlights hit us, they revealed a circle of four children and four adults, miles from pavement, under a moonless sky, heads bowed, hands joined in a tight circle. The car crept by and nearly slid off the opposite shoulder. As it wove back onto the road, we burst into laughter. Charlotte chuckled. "I can see the headline in the next *Axe Herald*: WITCHES' COVEN AT BLACK IRON LAKE." Giggling, we squeezed back into the vehicles and headed for Dairy Queen to celebrate the founding of our cult.

The next night Bert, Hunt, Milo, and I went down to

the north shore of Lake Attica to howl at the Olympus pack. The lake was so smooth that I could identify constellations on its surface. The Milky Way glowed like a streak of phosphorescence in a tropical sea. The air was cold and still, perfect for howling. Bert gestured us to a halt. While he set up his recording equipment, I clicked on the receiver and made a few slow sweeps with the antenna. Loud, irregular beeps told us that the radioed wolf, Hera of the Olympus pack, was directly across the lake from us, definitely within howling range. The signal seemed to be moving toward a single light that gleamed at the southwest corner of the lake. Bert began his howl, motioned us to join in, and clicked on the recorder as we trailed off, but not even a mosquito's whine marred the perfect silence.

We howled again, again without a reply. The radio signals steadied and remained at the same bearing. Suddenly a screen door slammed, the sound carrying undiminished across the lake. Flashlights bobbed and wove, and excited voices echoed hollowly. Bert cursed and clicked off the recorder. "Might as well go home." As we hiked back to the road, Hunt said he wanted to stop at the lodge across the lake where the door had slammed. A pair of Forest Service helicopter pilots were staying there, and he needed to talk to them.

We pulled into the resort to find a large Bell helicopter, rotors drooping, parked in the center of the lot. As we entered the lodge, Hunt was greeted by the bartender and two patrons, presumably the pilots, all talking at once. Hunt patted air with both hands. "One at a time, please," he asked. The bartender, gesticulating wildly with a bottle of Grain Belt, explained that they had just heard "ten wolves, at least, howling right outside the lodge." No sooner had they run outside than a moose, "pursued by at least a dozen wolves," had galloped across the parking lot. Exchanging glances heavy with mock concern, Milo, Bert, and I stepped outside.

Because the parking lot was completely dark, we turned the vehicle so the headlights flooded the lot. Although the surface was soft, there were no tracks, moose or wolf. Milo got the receiver and took a bearing on the wolf. The signal came from the east, about where it had been before. "I don't think he's moved," Milo said.

"Those wolves must have been the flying kind that don't leave tracks," offered Bert.

After Hunt and his family had left the next morning, Bert and I set up an antenna tower on Olympus Mountain, the highest point in the vicinity. The tower would allow us to get bearings on some of the nearer radioed wolves at times when flying was impossible. Though not really a mountain at all, Olympus Mountain was more than a hill. Its summit provided a commanding view of the forest from the Gantry mine in the west to the high logged-over ridges to the east.

With the antenna in place, it was time for a test. We got Freya, then Hera of the Olympus pack, still near Lake Attica, but couldn't pick up Ann of the Beach Lake pack. As we scribbled wolf numbers, bearings, and signal strengths, I asked Bert if he'd ever thought of using the radioed wolves' names on the forms. "It might be less confusing, and Hunt uses names with us," I added.

"Yeah," Bert replied. "I mentioned that to Hunt early this summer. He said it would interfere with our objectivity, that we'd be tempted to anthropomorphize. After a while, though, I noticed I was developing an affection for the numbers, too."

"I know what you mean. Freya isn't just any name any

more. Now it would seem really silly to call her any other name. Speaking of names, I notice we both refer to our leader as 'Hunt.' When do we get to call him 'Tom'? We've known him almost a year."

"How about now?" Bert replied. "Unless we can find out Charlotte's pet name for him. I asked her, but she wouldn't tell me, so it must be pretty awful."

"That's all the leverage we need. 'Tom' it is."

Bert and I spent the afternoon driving along old logging roads in the Olympus pack's territory.

At dusk we stopped on Route 3 near the place Freya had been when we located her from Olympus Mountain. We were quite close, so Bert began to unpack his equipment. As he struggled with his parabolic mike, headlights shone around the bend behind us. As the lights fell full upon our jeep, the oncoming vehicle squealed to a stop. Leaving his truck in the middle of the road, a fat, unshaven, crew-cut figure stumbled toward us, a ball peen hammer in his hand. He slurred an irate query about our business. Bert, ever the naïf, replied with the truth. The drunk staggered toward him, taking a fresh grip on his hammer. I disconnected the receiver, jammed the antenna through the tailgate, and ran to the driver's side of the jeep. I jumped in and hit the ignition in one motion, shouting to Bert to get in. He was already in, having hurled himself and his parabola through the tailgate. "Go! Go!" he screamed. The engine caught, and I dumped the clutch. The jeep's acceleration seemed even feebler than usual. Our attacker yelled something about "wolf lovers," and something hard hit the jeep's rear fender. "The hammer," Bert said, giggling hysterically.

In the mirror I saw the truck's headlights dim as the driver hit the starter. We were now flat-out at the jeep's maximum speed, about sixty. "There's an old logging road on the right at the bottom of the next hill," said Bert as he climbed forward into the passenger seat.

"Got it," I replied, crashing down into second gear. "Hang on." I cut the lights as we slid onto the logging road, which as I remembered was straight for a few hundred yards.

I brought the jeep to a stop by double-clutching into first and cutting the ignition, so our brake lights wouldn't give us away. The truck whizzed by.

I rested my forehead on the steering wheel. "Next time we're tracking satellites, OK?"

Bert nodded. "As long as we're here, why don't you drive to the top of the hill? That should put us within a few hundred yards of Freya." I was able to get a signal without the antenna while Bert set up his equipment. There was almost a minute of silence after he had howled. Then, somewhere off to the right, a twig snapped. The signal was strong with no antenna and the gain all the way down. There was a sharp, low bark, close enough to make me flinch. Bert pointed his parabola toward the bark, holding it, I thought, like a shield. There was another bark, louder than the first, then the crunch of footsteps, going away. Bert clicked the recorder to rewind.

"Did you get those barks?" I whispered. Bert passed me his earphones. There were the barks, in high fidelity. I checked the signal. It was fading fast. Already I needed a knife in the antenna socket to pick it up at all.

"Some night," said Bert. "Assaulted by a wolf hater and surrounded by a wolf."

The next night Bert was howling from the side of the road when an inquisitive logger stopped to inquire about the parabola. "Doing a radiation survey. Uranium," Bert explained. The logger grunted and drove on. Thus encouraged, Bert came up with a new cover story for each inquiry. As the summer wore on, Bert's ingenuity instigated a competition in which he, Milo, and I vied for the most outrageous lie to inquisitive passersby. I variously claimed to be monitoring signals from Russian spy satellites for the CIA, tuning in to live broadcasts of the Northton Symphony, and picking up radio signals from Comet Kohoutek, then on its overrated approach to earth. Milo stuck with animals, claiming to have radio collars on deer, moose, ducks, and shrews. Bert emerged victorious, however, with his straight-faced explanation to a group of tourists from Texas that he was picking up cosmic rays, focusing them with devices that looked like earphones but weren't, and directing them at a small tumor near the center of his brain. Not only did he avoid argument and assault, but one of the Texans wanted to buy stock in his invention if it worked.

I had hoped to gather some data on summer scent marking, but even on dusty roads it proved impossible to detect every mark, so I spent the long days of early August on my conditioning experiment, which proceeded slowly. Lotte, having chewed the reinforced Mark II into splinters, continued to test the strength of the Mark III. Gray would never get near any of the machines, so I worked only with Red, who pressed the bar enthusiastically but seemed unwilling or unable to learn the simplest discrimination of all: With or without odor that signaled reward, he pumped the bar at the same rate.

Fortunately I was able vicariously to enjoy Bert's success, for August was a month of nightly howls and he was getting replies almost half the time.

Bert howled whenever the wind was still, which was

generally at night. Since he was usually out long past midnight, he usually slept late, but one morning in mid-August I found him at the kitchen table changing batteries. He explained that he was trying to get some variety in his howling times in order to see if there were times of the day when wolves were most likely to respond. He was on his way to the Olympus pack's rendezvous site, he continued, and I was welcome to join him. The Olympus site was our favorite, because we could drive almost to the place where we howled and because the wolves, safely surrounded by swamp, were often willing to get quite close before they howled back, but we hadn't been there in more than a week. I decided that Red could use a day off and went with Bert.

The sun came up as we passed Olympus Mountain. Nearing the turnoff to the rendezvous site we could see that something had happened to the trees. In the bright horizontal sunbeams the birches were yellow, gold, and brown. A premature autumn had settled on the forest, but only on the south side of the road. Even as we speculated about how cold air might have flowed down off Olympus Mountain, we knew we were clutching at straws. Then, in the distance, we heard the chop-chop-chop of a helicopter and had the explanation. Our imaginative friends from Lake Attica had sprayed the defoliant 2,4-D around the site.

We drove slowly, evaluating various schemes for disabling helicopters. To our mixed relief and dismay, radio signals showed that two of the wolves, at least, were still there.

Wanting to spend as little time as possible in the area, I immediately began to check the many trails that led into the rendezvous site for sign. It had been my impression on our previous visits in the dark that there was an extraordinary number of scats on these trails, even considering how frequently they were used. Sure enough, every trail had its assembly of large scats. I counted seven in a six-foot circle on the main trail. A wolf or wolves must have exerted considerable control to place that many in the same place. At the junction of this trail with an old logging road I found another group of scats, this one containing eight. An hour of exploration convinced me that every trail in the vicinity was similarly marked. There was no way to walk near that rendezvous site without encountering several impressive advertisements of the presence of wolves. Since the adults were bringing food to the pups, some of the density of sign was due simply to the fact that a lot of meat was being eaten nearby, but whatever the motivation, the Olympus pack had left plenty of notice that it was around.

I was on my way back to meet Bert when the swamp behind me erupted into yips, barks, and squeals, which were suddenly cut off by a low growl. I could imagine the pups frisking around, working themselves up until one began to howl, the others joining in, and an adult shushing them. I froze to listen for a reply. A moment later there was a low howl from the east, definitely not Bert. I stayed where I was. Bert would not want to record my crunching progress during an antiphonal howl. The low howl came again, this time closer. I slowly sat down. After ten minutes that seemed like thirty, all hell broke loose in the swamp. The wolf with the low howl must have returned. I waited for a few minutes, then walked back to the road, finding a wolf print superimposed on one of my own tracks. The two prints, the wolf's and mine, were exactly the same width.

Bert was beaming. He'd got the whole thing on tape. He insisted on replaying it three times before we left to call "Tom" about the spraying.

Hunt said he'd do what he could, but it was already too late. The rendezvous site would soon be leafless. However, as far as he knew, 2,4-D was not highly toxic, and the pack would be leaving the site soon anyway. The pups were already able to keep up with the adults well enough to allow the whole pack to hunt together. Bert took it all quite well, considering that this rendezvous site was by far the easiest one to get to.

Bert's resignation was characteristic; his phlegmatic temper was well suited to a project with a relatively low rate of return on time invested. Although in August he was getting replies almost half the time, in early summer, when there were defenseless young pups at the dens, his response rate had been zero. Nevertheless, he had been out every night, yelling his lungs out, patiently recording mosquitoes and frogs. Since Bert howled only to wolves the radio signals of which came from within earshot, failure to get a reply when he knew there were wolves nearby must have been doubly frustrating, but Bert never showed a sign of discouragement.

Toward the end of August Bert acted on a rare impulse and howled when there were no radioed wolves nearby. He was at the Linde Lake lookout east of Axe. "There was no wind, and it seemed like a good place for a howl," he later explained. The reply he received vindicated his intuition. When he played it back for us, there was for once none of the banal banter with which men disguise their feelings. No one was willing to betray the perfection of the song. A single wolf moaned in a tenor register, dropped down a fifth, returned, dropped again, returned, and

131

dropped a diminished fifth. How little that description says about how the howl sounded. We'll never know what the wolf was expressing but it doesn't matter: To me the howl, which Paul Winter used in his album *Common Ground*, was a perfect statement of everything I had ever felt or would feel about wolves and the wilderness of which they are a part.

9
Hunts

Echoes of that howl followed me all the way back to Ann Arbor, where all too soon they were lost in the clamor of fall term. Raymond Bach, my dissertation chairman, could hold the committee responsible for my candidacy at bay no longer; I would have to take my preliminary Ph.D. exams before Thanksgiving. I spent most of the fall in the stacks of the graduate library and managed to pass my exams. I was, in the lingo of academia, A.B.D., All But Dissertation, a designation I could contemplate only with rue, for the document in question was then only a long strip of gas chromatograph tracings, a stack of illegible field notes, and an unopened box of Corrasable bond.

No matter. I would soon be back in the north. With a chuckle of regret, I sold my car to an unsuspecting law student and spent the proceeds on an elderly but sound panel truck. Into the truck went my books, stereo, and a pair of cross-country skis on which I hoped to travel faster than on snowshoes. By mid-December the truck's knobby snow tires were thrumming the snowpacked highways of the Upper Peninsula. I drove through Baraga at dusk and climbed out of the foggy shroud of the Great Lakes in the dark. At the bottom of every hollow, pockets of frozen air stiffened the suspension and steering, a subtle but chilling hint of how cold it was.

The driveway to the lab had been plowed, making a tunnellike entrance, the walls of which were taller than the truck. Yellow lights glowed in the windows of the lodge. Snow squeaked beneath my boots. I opened the door of the lodge only enough to admit me and my pack and slammed it against the cold. Bert was at the kitchen table, changing the batteries on a receiver. Before I could ask where Freya was, he had already answered.

"She's on the ridge above the lab, about a quarter of a mile south. Probably right off Winter Camp Road. Tom collared her mate and pups. Her mate's Frey, and the pups are Odin and Loki."

After stowing my gear, I returned to the kitchen to talk with Bert. When he left for a midnight howling session, I threw another log onto the fire and watched the flames' reflections flicker on the ceiling for a while before I slid into sleep.

Sun struck the wolves as they lay in a snow hollow beneath a jack pine's sagging branches. The smoke-colored female opened one eye, blinked, then opened the other. Slowly she raised her head and sniffed the still air. She yawned hugely, then rose and stretched each leg in turn. She was hungry.

There was a flicker of motion on the shore of the lake below. The female froze as a deer walked out onto the lake. Perhaps it was only a change in her breathing that wakened the male, but it was as though an electric current had passed through the snow. His eyes snapped open,

134

hisnostrils quivered, and he drew his legs beneath him. The deer stopped and looked back over its shoulder as another deer tiptoed out of the forest. Haltingly the pair turned to walk along the shore toward the waiting wolves. When they were thirty yards away, the female leaped forward. In four strides she was at top speed, back flexing, rear legs reaching past the front as they stretched, grabbed, and whipped the snow into a mist that showered the male as he slowly overtook her. His strides grew longer until his tautly strung sinews reached resonance like strings coming into tune, flexing in unison with his lungs' diapason.

The deer didn't hesitate; by the time the female had completed her first stride, they were bounding for the trees. They reached the forest edge in five bounds, while the wolves took eight. The snow was deep in the forest, deep enough to cover the logs and rocks that the deer leaped over with ease, leaving a trail of elongated craters. The male could not quite leap from one crater to the next; after each bound he floundered in chest-high snow. The sounds of the deer grew fainter as he lunged, but their scent hung in the air.

The female took the lead. Her mate had broken trail, so she was still strong, and they soon closed in on their quarry. The wolves burst into a clearing. Each lunge was now a separate effort. One of the deer stood on the other side, stretching its neck to browse.

Rested, the deer bounced away, still chewing its mouthful of spruce tips. Lurching to a halt, the wolves stood panting, watching with unblinking eyes as its tail wigwagged away into the trees. Their breaths returned quickly. They touched noses, turned, and retraced their trail to the shore.

It was still dark when I headed out the next morning, and I paused to enjoy the starlight on the snow. There was no moon, but there was enough light to read the thermometer: twenty-two below. Dense with cold, the air felt almost liquid. It burned my throat and filled my lungs. Exhilarated, I felt I could leap tall jack pines, outrun a deer, terrify a wolf with my howl. Freya was on the ridge, and there was no one around, so this last fancy, at least, could be effected. I howled. Terrified or not, Freya replied before I could draw my next breath. Frey and the pups joined in. I could not have asked for a better welcome.

With the Upsala Lake pack less than half a mile away there was no need to drive. I didn't have to gather my notebook, compass, map, matches, and knife; my day pack had been ready for weeks. I knew that skis would be awkward in bush, so I strapped a pair of snowshoes to my pack and was off.

There was a hint of light in the east as I skied across the icy parking lot and double-poled out to the highway. A trace of windblown snow covered both shoulders, perfect for taking tracks. At the top of the hill I found them. Heading west, the Upsala Lake pack had cut the corner between Birch Road and Winter Camp Road. It had saved a quarter of a mile or so by taking a hypotenuse through a small spruce swamp. I recorded the maneuver, and, not wishing to disturb the wolves, whose howls had come from only a few hundred yards away, I began to follow their tracks backward along Birch Road. They had trotted along the road for about a mile, leaving RLUs in pairs, one a thin, wiggly line, the other a dense spray.

As long as I stayed on the road, the skis were an enormous improvement over showshoes, and where I left the road to follow the tracks across another swamp, I found

136

that even in deep powder they worked at least as well as snowshoes. At the rate I was going I should be able to gather twice as many data as I had the winter before.

The trail led me off the road and through the forest. Emerging from the trees, the wolf trail skirted the edge of a large swamp, making a large semicircle. Why hadn't the wolves cut straight across? Reminding myself that I was backtracking, I stopped at the other side of the swamp, turned, and faced the way the wolves had headed. This did not help. Perhaps they were using the trees as cover; it seems that wolves do hunt whenever they travel. I made a quick sketch and resumed my backward journey.

At the edge of the swamp one of the wolves had deposited a scat, nearly buried in the trench they had plowed through the fluffy powder. Upon examination it proved to be a mouse that had evidently been swallowed whole and excreted nearly intact. Its streamlined fecal form was not very different from its natural shape, but its odor left little doubt that it had passed through a wolf: It had the familiar sweet-sour pungency of anal gland secretions. I wrapped the murine Jonah in a sandwich bag and placed it in my pack.

The trail led into a birch forest and then veered north, back toward Birch Road. Half an hour later I jumped off a snowbank onto the road and recorded my first RLU in two miles. There were three more RLUs in the next mile, all on the snowbanks that lined the road. Why, I wondered, had they been so profligate along the road and then refrained from scent marking in the bush? Because intruders would be more likely to use the road? Because it's hard to raise a leg when you're belly-deep in powder? In order to befuddle novice ethologists?

The wolves had entered the road from a snowmobile

trail that led to the north. Any irritation I might once have felt at snowmobilers' noisy violations of the forest's silence vanished as I picked up speed on the trail. Two inches of dry snow had fallen on the well-packed base, providing ideal conditions for skiing and for tracking. With any luck the trail would go all the way to the river. If so, I could ski back along the Ontolagon without retracing my route.

I was warm from exertion, and the sun was at its zenith, but it was cold enough to justify a fire when I stopped for lunch. It didn't take long for a gray jay to home in on the smoke. I traded a sardine for the latest bird gossip and tidied up my notes. When my lunch was consumed, the jay left with mercenary dispatch. I reluctantly kicked snow over the friendly flames, snapped boots into bindings, and got back to work. The Ontolagon River, which marked the northern boundary of the Upsala Lake pack's territory, could not be far, and it was unlikely the wolves would cross it. Perhaps the tracks would take me back toward the lab. If not, I'd have to leave them at the river. I wasn't sure how fast I'd be able to go, and I wanted to be back at the lab by dusk. Not a soul knew where I was, and the afternoon sun was already diving toward the treetops, taking the temperature with it.

After another half mile there was no sign of the river, nor had the trail begun to descend, as I knew it must when it entered the river valley. A vague anxiety soon gave way to annoyance when I saw that the wolves had not followed the snowmobile trail all the way from the river. Two yellow stains marked their emergence from a dense thicket of alders and beaked hazels. Reluctant to enter the thicket, I shuffled down the trail until I'd assured myself that this was no mere excursion and that they really had reached the trail through the brush.

I exchanged skis for snowshoes and, with the skis on my back snagging branches at every step, slogged and crashed through the tangle.

Unable to see more than a few yards ahead, I was at first unaware that I had begun to descend. Then, without warning, I found myself atop a tiny cliff with the reedy shore of the frozen Ontolagon visible directly below through the webs of my snowshoes. I shook my head in amazement and then for the first time since lunch checked my compass. The trail through the brush had been straight. The river should be off to the right, not directly ahead. The compass confirmed my opinion. Was this some uncharted river? Not likely, but I was facing only slightly north of west, and the river ran east and west, didn't it? I consulted my map. A glance showed me what had happened. In the months since my last work in the north my memory had, like a psychological Corps of Engineers, rectified the river so that it ran east and west.

The dismay I felt at the inadequacy of my own mental map was quickly replaced by admiration for the wolves', for they had left the easy going on the river at its closest approach to the snowmobile trail, which was half a mile away on the other side of a cliff and thick brush, and had taken the shortest route to the trail. Evidently their knowledge of local terrain was better than my own. Of course, it was possible that they had followed old signs or taken the shortcut by chance, but as I remembered from the flight sheets at the lab, they hadn't been in this part of their territory for weeks. I made a note to find some way to determine how long the odors of scent marks last, so I could tell when wolves might be following odor trails and when they had to depend on memory alone.

From my vantage point atop the cliff I could see that the wolves had come up the river for some distance. I'd be able to get more data on my way back to the lab. Once I'd made my way to the bottom and exchanged snowshoes for skis, I again made excellent time, and I arrived at the lab fifteen scent marks richer.

I reflected on Lloyd Morgan's canon, a dictum from one of the first modern students of animal behavior which required that simple explanations like scent trails and rote learning be eliminated before complex ones like insight could be used to explain shortcuts like that afternoon's. Why was Morgan's dour skepticism less appealing than mental maps? Was it only because the simpler hypotheses couldn't handle the facts without some awfully complex finagling, or was I still struggling in the anthropomorphic clutches of the Naked Wolf?

Two sets of tracks lay like rails across the frozen lake. At their vanishing point two wolves loped, shadowless under the full moon. Sounds of breathing, sounds of snow squeaking beneath their feet. Their breaths plumed, condensed into powdery snow, and fell out of the frozen air. They did not feel the cold around them any more than they saw the stars overhead.

The lake narrowed, and they slowed to a walk. Water gurgled beneath the ice, almost drowning a distant wail. The female turned toward the shore, moving more quickly. The male followed at a trot. The next howl was louder, a pandemonium of yips, shrieks, and moans. The male's hackles went up. He growled softly, and his teeth flashed briefly. His tongue flicked over his curling lip. They turned and headed the other way, two shadows moving among the shadows along the shore.

I was at the Transbush Airways base at Windy Point at

dawn, installing antennas while Sam checked the oil, gas, and control surfaces. The skis were frozen to the ice, so I stood in the prop blast and yanked a strut while Sam gave it full throttle. When the skis popped free, I swung aboard and climbed in. Minutes later we homed in on Freya. She and the rest of her pack were still on the ridge above the lab, gnawing on the remains of a deer. She looked up as we circled. For a moment I thought she wagged her tail, but soon I decided it must have been a trick of the slanting morning light. I pointed east toward the Stabler Lake pack.

Sam straightened us out, trimmed to climb, and nudged the throttle. Suddenly he stiffened, turned up the volume on the two-way radio, and grabbed the mike. Somehow he'd picked up something relevant from the constant murmur of voices and crackle of static. He gave our aircraft number and asked for a repeat. After a few seconds he turned to ask if we still had some radioed packs along Arquebus Trail.

"I don't know. Where is it?" I asked as I spread my map.

Sam pointed to a dotted line running northeast from the end of Muttberg Road. "Two skiers left from Wit's End the day before yesterday. They were supposed to meet their wives at Winipeg Lodge, but they never showed up. There's a search on."

I quickly counted the one-mile squares on the map. "That's almost thirty miles. Not a bad two-day trip."

"They were traveling light. No tents, no stoves; just bags and four meals of freeze-dried. They planned to make a snow cave. Can we try to find some wolves over that way?"

I thought quickly. I had hoped to find some tracks to follow that afternoon, but any we found in that part of the forest would be too far away; by the time I finished the wolf survey and drove to the end of the road, it would be well into the afternoon. On the other hand, my duties included a periodic check on all the radioed packs, not just the ones I could follow. And there was an ethic of the bush that said that when anyone was lost, you looked. Someday it might be you. There were at least two packs the territories of which lay more or less along Arquebus Trail. One hadn't been located in a week and had last been seen on Lake Finlandia. "Let's head for Fin," I said.

Sam took us up to 5,000 feet. As we roared along, I listened for the signals of radioed packs to the south, trying to get a rough idea of where to look later on. Between packs I wondered what it would be like to be lost down there. My own brief periods of disorientation, like the one the day before, were frightening enough. And I had been only a mile or so from the nearest road.

The first signals of the Mogul Lake pack came through the static, dead ahead. I motioned for a descent. This was one of the best parts of radio tracking: a long, shallow glide with the nose low, the pack invisible but down there somewhere, their signals stronger with every beep. I signaled for a slight correction to the left, worked the gain down as quickly as I could, then straightened us out again. Sam responded so quickly and smoothly it was as though through my gestures I were flying the plane, a Toscanini of the air.

The beeps crescendoed. I lowered the gain all the way and heard them even louder. I pointed straight down. Sam cut the throttle. The plane dropped. I flicked the antenna switch, heard the beeps louder on the right, and pointed. The right wing dipped, and I was looking straight down at a pack of five sprawled along a ridge in postures of limp relaxation. "Right down the stack," I said. "Where the hell are we?"

We climbed to get our bearings, and as the nearest lakes came into view, I marked the pack's position. There was a hole in Hunt's mosaic of radioed packs to the north, so he'd instructed me to look for wolf tracks whenever a flight took me there. We'd had reports of a pair of wolves in the hole, one coal black, the other pure white. One of our pilots, who'd seen hundreds of wolves from the air but never a black one, had promised us a double snap roll if we could find it. The promise of acrobatics added little to Hunt's desire to find the wolves, for he regarded un-radioed packs in his study area with something akin to lust. A few sightings of tracks would give him some idea about where to set his traps, so I decided to kill two birds with one stone: We could look for wolf tracks and ski tracks at the same time. I asked for a search pattern, an elongated rectangular spiral with the long axis over Arquebus Trail. Sam kept us at about 3,500 feet, high enough for a good view but low enough to allow us to identify tracks.

Less than a week had passed since the last snowfall, but little of the wintry register was left unsigned; only the frozen lakes were unmarked. Each set of tracks was as distinctive as a signature: the scribbled autographs of moose; the delicate dots and dashes of walking and running deer; the cursive calligraphy of beavers sliding from lodge to shore and back. But nowhere was there the determined rectilinearity that was the hallmark of human or wolf.

We flew over an old beaver pond, now a tree-sprinkled marsh. Its surface had been inscribed with the long, dragging strokes of a slowly moving moose. Moose tracks are always somewhat erratic, but they usually show at least a lackadaisical sort of herbivorous purpose as they meander from shrub to shrub. These did not. They were a tangled skein that went nowhere. Sam banked to circle the marsh, then pointed down the wing. A large antlerless moose stood in the shade at the eastern edge.

"Brainworm," he said, referring to a parasite that in one of its several incarnations moves through a moose's nasal membranes into the brain. "One of my pilots had an infected moose stick his antlers into the prop. They are nothing to mess with. Take a look." The moose lunged forward, striking out with a foreleg at some invisible enemy, then whirled and kicked again. Soon, I hoped, a real wolf would replace the hallucination and end the creature's misery. Sam took us back into our pattern.

The shore of Lake Superior was visible at the northern end of each sweep. On our third approach the sun was high behind us, making it easier to see tracks. A herringbone pattern laced the snow near the top of a bare ridge to the north. Sam banked and reached for the microphone at the same time. We flew along the ridge to an open slope where a pair of ski tracks wove graceful telemarks through deep powder. Sam made contact with Gresh, the flying warden who had buzzed me the previous winter. He announced our location and our intention to follow the tracks. They disappeared into dense forest at the bottom of the slope, so we flew in the direction they had been going.

We picked them up again on Minihaha Lake, a half mile or so to the west. The tracks lay north and south, and it was impossible to tell in which direction the skiers had gone. I suggested we land and look at the marks left by their ski poles, which should tilt in the direction of travel, but Sam pointed out that in the dry powder on the lake it might be impossible to detect any tilt. He radioed Gresh and said we'd follow the tracks south. Gresh could follow them north; he'd be at Minihaha Lake in five minutes.

We lost the trail in the forest south of the lake but picked them up again on the next lake to the south. These tracks gave me the same chill the moose's had. They were just as crazy. Skirting the northern shore, they split up, headed out to the middle, rejoined, and traced two separate but equally erratic courses back to the northern shore. We flew a spiral, hoping to pick them up again. Neither Sam nor I could imagine any rational explanation for the tracks. "Maybe they were arguing which way to go," I suggested. "Or maybe they were hypothermic."

A few minutes later Gresh was on the radio. He'd found the skiers. He declined Sam's offer of assistance. The skiers were half a mile from the nearest lake either of us could land on, so he'd radioed for a larger, faster plane and paramedics, who would be there by the time he'd got them out. We located another pack and headed back toward Olympus Mountain, eavesdropping on Gresh's conversation with the rescue flight.

"You won't believe this." His voice crackled. "One of them is completely bananas. He keeps talking about the carnival, says that's where his buddy is, at the carnival." There was a switching transient, a pause, and then Gresh was back. "He wants me to take him to the carnival to find his buddy. He'd burned his skis to stay warm and was getting ready to throw his parka into the fire when I got to him. I don't think his buddy is going to make it." I directed my attention back to the snow. High clouds thinned the light, but the sun was low enough to show tracks clearly. We swooped to get a look at a set of tracks on Winipeg Lake. They were straight enough to be wolf, and upon closer inspection that's what they proved to be.

Beyond them a flicker of motion caught my eye. What I saw made no sense. Snowshoe hare tracks were appearing beside the wolf trail, hop after hop, but there was no hare. Then I realized what was happening: a hare in winter pelage, invisible against the snow, was eclipsing its own shadow as it hopped across the lake. I pointed it out to Sam.

"Had you worried, there, huh?" I admitted that it had. The signals from the radioed wolves of the Olympus pack came from an enormous clearcut between Jack Pine Trail and Molly Loop. Thanks to the open terrain, I spotted the wolves before we flew over them. Four of them were walking west along an unplowed logging road. The leader urinated on a log, then scratched the snow with stiffened forelegs. Each of the others sniffed both marks. They continued down the road, evenly spaced, about twenty yards apart. Hoping for another episode of scent marking, I began to film their progress with my movie camera.

The lead wolf stopped, his nose in the air. The second wolf joined him, and they touched noses. Then the first wolf was off, running through deep snow at right angles to the road. A deer burst from a small patch of jack pine. The wolf had closed to within seventy yards when the deer disappeared into a clump of tall trees. When they emerged on the other side, the deer had increased its lead but began to arc to the left. The wolf cut across the arc and the second wolf, just emerging from the timber, followed. Our circle took us out of the line of sight, and when we came around again, the first wolf was gaining. The other two wolves, probably the pups, ran back and forth along the road, tails wagging furiously as they sniffed the snow. The deer came to a halt and turned to face the wolf, which accelerated, lunged, and grabbed it by the

146

nose. The deer leaped and yanked in vain. Predator and prey moved around each other in a circle until the second wolf rushed in from the side, struck the deer on the flank, and knocked it down. Then both wolves tore at its belly. A red stain crept across the snow. It took five more minutes for the other two wolves to join the killers, which had already chewed the deer nearly in half. Within twenty minutes the deer was a skeleton lying in a patch of bloody snow.

Sam tapped my shoulder, then the gas gauge. I got the message. We'd been in the air more than three hours. I had him make one more circle so I'd be sure to be able to find the place when I skied in that afternoon.

I listened for Freya again as we approached the lab. She had moved east and was directly below us. Since we were almost home, I asked Sam if we could have just one more circle. He shrugged and took us down. Just as the beeps began to come in loud, Sam dipped the left wing and pointed. Three deer were crossing a small swamp at full speed. Just before entering the trees, one of the deer stopped and looked back over its shoulder. A wolf plunged out of the woods and into the deep snow of the swamp. It didn't look much smaller than the deer, but it was having a much harder time, coming to a complete halt after every leap.

A second wolf, somewhat smaller than the first, appeared in the first wolf's tracks. The signals told me it was Freya. She was having greater difficulty than her mate even though he had broken trail. The lead wolf disappeared after the deer, and again she took up the chase.

A few moments later the pups emerged from the forest. Halfway across the swamp the first one stopped, sat, and licked a rear paw. It had probably gathered some ice. The second pup, running full tilt with its head down, collided

147

with the first. They both went sprawling off the trail into the deep, powdery snow. They floundered, almost swimming as they struggled back to the path made by the adults. One pup took off in pursuit, but the other pup, evidently disoriented by the collision, followed the trail in the wrong direction. Sam moved our circle to follow the chase. The deer were farther ahead now and moving more slowly. One of them stopped and nibbled briefly at a small white pine. The wolves plowed steadily on. The deer stood until they were only about 100 yards away, then bounded off as though the snow were no hindrance at all. The race was clearly lost, but the wolves kept coming. Only the first one was in the running. Freya had fallen behind, and the pup behind her, though gaining, had not caught up. The other pup was nowhere in sight.

Suddenly it was over. The lead wolf made one last bound, gathered himself for the next leap, but never made it. He simply stood. Even from the air the heaving of his flanks was visible. Freya came up behind him and flopped down onto her side. The pup behind her sniffed her rear, then lay down in the trail. Two hundred yards away the deer browsed peacefully.

When I returned to the lab, Hunt's car was in the lot. He had arrived a day early. I greeted his arrival with mixed emotions, for glad as I was to see him, I had not transcribed the flight sheets I'd filled out, nor had I filled in the descriptions of wolf locations in the legal terminology of township, range, and section that he required. As I feared, he was at the kitchen table, scowling over a stack of flight sheets, straight from the cockpit, scrawled as we bounced through air pockets or whirled in 3 g circles. We exchanged perfunctory greetings and went to work. "What's this?" he asked mildly, pointing to a form that placed the

148

Mogul Lake pack at the east edge of "Lqumbda Lake." "I know the lake names are a little strange around here, but they're not that strange."

"Let me look in my journal." I gulped. After some cross-checking, I was able to translate "Lqumbda" and several other impossibilities into real lakes and precise locations.

"You see why I want legal descriptions. The east shore of that lake is two miles long."

"Right. They were at T fifty-three N R three W section fifteen center."

He grunted and jotted the legal description down. After an hour of interrogation I vowed never to step from an airplane with an unfinished flight sheet. When the last of the forms had been neatly transcribed, and every pack's location pinned down, Hunt pushed back from the table, passed a hand over his pate, and said, "Let's eat."

Over dinner we talked about my data. I was able to report 150 RLUs, about half that number of SQUs and scats, and about 20 scratches. I attributed much of my progress to the use of skis as well as snowshoes, but Hunt was skeptical. He couldn't believe that there was anything better than the bear-paws he'd used all his life. Skis were toys, snowshoes tools, and that was that. I did not press the point.

At 5:30 A.M. Hunt padded through the kitchen, where I was sipping coffee and working on my notes. He stepped outside to check the weather, a ritual he performed every day we flew. I could have told him it was still and clear, but he would have checked anyway. I closed my notebook and gulped the last of my coffee, for I knew that when he came back, he'd say we'd better get going. He did. I refrained from pointing out that I was fully dressed, and he still in pajamas, knowing the incredible speed with which he could prepare to leave. By the time I'd gathered the flight kit, binoculars, and my pack, slid into my parka, and grabbed some sandwiches, he was fully dressed and on his way to the door.

In response to that winter's gasoline crisis, Hunt had bought a Toyota, which he drove with gusto. Ralph Louis's flying was sedate by comparison. Seconds after we had taken off, Louis began a steep bank that threatened to drag a wing on the ice.

We located two packs along Muttberg Road, then headed north. As we flew over the strait at a place mysteriously named Desert Portage, Hunt asked Louis to take us down. At first I could see only a black patch of open water, probably caused by rapid flow through the straits, but as we descended, I noticed two elongate forms on the adjacent shore. I wiped the frost from the window and saw that they were wolves. There was something in the water just in front of them. I readied my movie camera. We spiraled lower and lower. With my camera zoomed to maximum magnification I could see that the object in the water was a deer.

The deer had gained only a temporary sanctuary by entering the water, for now it was trapped. The water was deep on one side of the hole, and the wolves waited on the other. Time after time the deer swam to the side away from the wolves, until it finally got a foreleg onto the ice. Immediately one of the wolves ran around the open water, avoiding the thin ice at its edges, and stood in front of the deer. The section of ice under the deer's leg broke loose, and once again it floundered. How long could it last, I wondered, in water that was well below freezing, kept fluid only by the current? Which would it choose,

150

freezing to death or being ripped open by a wolf? The latter would be more logical. Death in the water was certain, and with only one wolf on the shore there would be a slight chance of escape.

As though it had just reached the same conclusion, the deer lunged ashore, but it had been so weakened by the cold that as it entered the shallows, its drive ended in a feeble splash. The wolf on the shore struck, knocked the deer back into the water, then waded in, grabbed the deer by the neck, and dragged it onto the shore. The deer struggled to get up, but the wolf was already tearing at its belly. The other wolf joined it, and in the tug-of-war that ensued, the deer was dragged in a bloody arc across the snow.

Hunt asked Louis to take us to Washtenaw Lake, where I'd located but not seen the radioed members of the Russian Lake pack the previous day. As soon as he'd got a fix on one of the wolves, Hunt turned to ask, "Is this about where they were yesterday?"

"This is exactly where they were yesterday," I said. "T fifty-one, R one W, section seven northwest," I added smugly.

After circling the deer in the water, we had barely enough fuel to complete the survey, so after circling only long enough to pinpoint the signals, we flew on to Neptune Lake to find the next pack.

An ancient drama was being played on the frozen lake. From our height the actors themselves were nearly invisible, so it was their shadows that we watched. Grotesquely elongated by the low morning sun, the shadow of a deer floated across the snow. Close behind was the El Greco silhouette of a running wolf. The wolf shadow was closing fast. The deer shadow changed shape as it veered, but it was too late. The shadows fused.

151

Wind whined in the struts as Louis put us into a side-slip. Suddenly we were watching the players themselves. The deer struggled to its feet, only to be hauled down by the wolf once again. The wolf released its grip on a haunch, then struck again, this time from the side. A red stain spread. The wolf and its shadow raised their heads as though to howl.

Within a few minutes three other wolves converged on the kill, one from the east side of the lake, the other two from the west. The wolf at the kill charged at the new-comer from the east and chased it off to the north. By the time the first wolf returned to the kill, the other two wolves had already begun to feed. All three tore at the carcass side by side until one of them pulled off a leg.

"Not much strategy there," I said. "I've been reading about cutting the prey off as a form of strategy, but it looked to me as if the wolf were oriented toward the deer all the time."

"There might have been some strategy involved in catching the deer out on the ice in the first place," Hunt replied. "Deer can usually outrun wolves in the forest."

"Do you suppose the others were waiting for the one that got the deer to chase it onto the lake? If he hadn't got it, they might have. And what about the wolf that got chased away—do you think he was from another pack?"

"Maybe to both questions," said Hunt over his shoulder. Then to Louis: "Let's go to Lake Vaarna."

Two hours later we were back at the lab. It was too late to get to the nearest tracks, so I paid a visit to Lotte, Red, and Gray. By dusk I'd lost two buttons, a bootlace, and a glove, my hat was in shreds, and I was covered with mud. Mercifully Joe invited me in, and soon the cheery warmth of his fire was matched by the inner glow of his aquavit. We traded tales of youth and foolishness for an hour or so. As I left, he wished me Merry Christmas. In the isolation of fieldwork and the frenzy of Hunt's visit I had forgotten that it was Christmas Eve.

10

Trespasses

For wolves the twenty-fifth of December is just another day. There are no presents to open; dinner, if there is any, will be elusive; and callers are as unwelcome as ever. For me the day was similarly undistinguished. As usual, I was up before dawn, driven from my bed not by the spirit of the season or devotion to science but by the threat of frostbite. I started a fire, threw on a parka, jammed on my boots, and went outside to plug in the jeep. It did not feel much colder outside than in, but according to the thermometer, it was sixteen below. The only sound was the gentle hiss of falling snow.

By the time I was ready to leave, the snow had stopped and the sky had cleared. The sun, just over the horizon, was already starting tiny avalanches in the treetops, cascades that whispered, then whooshed as loads of powder fell from bough to bough and finally thumped heavily into a soft white cushion below.

Freya's signal came from north of Birch Road, so my plan was to drive to the Outward Bound camp and ski along the river until I cut her trail. About a quarter of a mile down the camp road I spotted several sets of wolf and one of deer tracks. A chain of dime-sized pink spatters lay between the deer tracks. I parked the jeep by ramming it into the snowbank—I could worry about getting it out later—and walked up the road far enough to assure myself that the pink spots were not brake or automatic transmission fluid, both of which had fooled me before. They were not, unless the deer had brakes or an automatic transmission, for atop the snowbank on the edge of the road, where the deer must have stood for a moment before jumping down, was a patch of bright red the size of my hand.

Just in case the wolves had the deer down nearby I decided to backtrack north toward the Ontolagon River. I could visit the kill, if there were one, later, after the wolves had had their meal. I followed the tracks back down a gentle slope, finding spots of blood almost as far as the shore, where three sets of running wolf tracks met the tracks of a running deer. A tuft of deer hair attached to a small patch of hide lay on the snow where the tracks converged.

The river was wide, shallow, and windswept. The wolves had fanned out as they crossed, running easily on the thin layer of well-packed snow that covered the ice. One had stayed on the course taken by the deer, two to one side, and at least two more to the other. There had to be at least five wolves, and the Upsala Lake pack had only four, so these tracks must have been made by members of the Beach Lake pack to the north. I had just received the perfect Christmas present: a trespass at a time when the resident pack was nearby, leaving scent marks the intruders were sure to find. For the first time I'd be able to examine responses to fresh foreign sign. The possibility of face-to-face contact between the packs was too remote to consider, but these tracks were fresh, and Freya was not very far away.

I returned to the jeep and tried to pick up Freya's signal. I couldn't get it, so she was not as close as I had thought. I wouldn't have to worry about chasing her away from Christmas dinner. The northern pack was a different matter. I didn't want to affect their behavior, but going ahead was a risk I had to take. If I waited to let them move on of their own accord, I might lose their tracks under another snowstorm—clouds were already piling up in the west.

The wounded deer's route took it into a region of thickly wooded ridges, so I proceeded on snowshoes. The spots of blood were larger and more frequent than before, but the deer's strides were still long as it descended into a swampy bay to the south of the Outward Bound camp. Once across the bay, the wolves were out of the narrow fringe of common use that surrounds wolf territories and into the core of the Upsala Lake pack's domain.

The tracks led up a steep hill on the south side of the bay, and for five minutes I brachiated, pulling myself hand over hand from branch to branch. From the top of the hill the tracks continued south for a quarter of a mile, veered abruptly, and then doubled back to head north. Two RLUs, a scat, and a scratch marked the change of course. The wolves had given up. Their aversion to the Upsala Lake pack's territory had evidently outweighed their desire to chase a deer, even one they had already wounded. Before I could conclude that hunger had been overridden by fear, however, I would have to see how far the deer had gone. Perhaps the deer was in better shape than it seemed; many chases end with wolves giving up for reasons that have nothing to do with territoriality.

I continued after the deer, but I didn't have far to go. Within 100 yards of where the wolves had turned there was a pool of blood almost half a yard across. Though cold, it was not yet frozen. Another 100 yards on, I found the deer itself. Half its haunch had been torn open. It was hard to believe a deer in that condition could have moved at all, much less run more than a mile, but there was no other sign around. The wound must have been inflicted by the trespassers.

The Upsala Lake pack could not be far away, so I did not disturb the deer. If only they could find it, their Christmas dinner had been delivered. Should I howl? I decided against it. A howl from me would be as likely to drive them away as to attract them to the kill, and the trespassers might still be within range of my voice.

The trespassers had traveled single file back to the river, then fanned out as they started across. The river was narrower here than where they had crossed before, and steep banks provided some protection from the wind. I could see every footprint clearly. There were four trails at first. Then one of the trails split, and split again. It looked as though another of the trails had split near the middle of the river. I needed only to check that last set of tracks to get an exact count of the number of trespassers. I slogged out onto the ice.

A muffled crunch came from the ice all around me. In sickening slow motion I sank into the black water that flooded the hole I made. Suddenly the ice beneath my showshoes was whipped away by the current, and I dropped in to my armpits. My snowshoes were being yanked downstream, and for a moment my face went under. I kicked convulsively in an attempt to release my feet, but the bindings held. I flung my arms onto the ice and clawed, but to no avail. The current was sucking me back down. I hammered for a handhold but succeeded only in breaking off a piece of ice the size of a card table. It began to tilt. My legs were already so numb I couldn't tell if they were kicking. I considered ducking underwater to remove my snowshoes, but once drawn beneath the ice, I would have no hope of getting back to the hole.

If only I could get a grip on the ice, I could wriggle out. In my pocket was my knife, secured by a lanyard to a belt loop. I removed one hand from the ice to reach for the knife and began to slide even faster. I yanked at the lanyard, and the belt loop gave. Still clawing with my left hand, I opened the larger blade with my teeth and drove it into the ice as hard as I could. Miraculously it held. With both hands on the knife I was able to pull the upper half of my body onto the ice. By repeatedly lifting the knife out and driving it back into the ice an inch or two farther away, I pulled myself until I lay across the chunk of ice. Once my snowshoes were out of the water, I slashed the bindings and pulled them out of the water. I slid along on my belly, using the snowshoes to support my weight until I was sure I was on firm ice, then stood on them and shuffled to shore. Now I knew why the wolves had spread out to cross the river.

A fallen spruce provided plenty of resinous wood for a bonfire, and I had matches in a waterproof container. Soon I was stripped, turning like a side of meat to stay warm as my clothes steamed on overhanging branches. It took an hour for them to dry to the point where they were slightly better than no clothes at all. I repaired my bindings but did not fasten them until I had shuffled gingerly across the river.

Approaching the last separation in the tracks from the other side, I saw that there were indeed seven sets. Since I was already on the north side of the river, I followed the trespassers for another mile or so to see where they had gone after their frustrating experience with the deer. They had made a beeline into the core of their own territory, scent-marking heavily all along the way. Reluctantly I turned back.

Halfway back to the jeep, I began to feel light-headed. I found a snow-free bowl beneath a huge spruce and sat in its cozy shelter to eat a salted nut roll. The cold was no longer oppressive. In fact, it was pleasant. It ordered the northern air and brought logic to the molecular commotion, creating a great clear crystal. Absolute perfection could exist only at absolute zero, for there alone do entropy and organization find their frozen union. I fell back into the soft snow and waved my arms and legs to make a snow angel. I rolled slow thoughts around behind closed eyes. For the first time in hours my feet were not cold. What was the hurry? What was it that I had been so uptight about? Something to do with wolves, no doubt. Somehow that seemed very funny.

I have no idea how long I sat there in hypothermic euphoria or what brought me to my senses. It might have been the sound of my own laughter, for the idea of following wolves around, scribbling notes, and wearing great, galumphing snowshoes seemed hilarious. I remember struggling to remind myself of something important that had nothing to do with wolves or snowshoes but had to do with skis and a carnival. Suddenly I realized that I had to get moving again, though I couldn't remember why. I began to play the cold morning game: resolving to get up in just one more minute, then in one minute more. It was probably pure habit that got me to my feet.

My fingers were too numb to tie my makeshift bindings, so I shuffled along with only my toes engaged until I'd generated enough body heat to work my hands. Somehow I headed in the right direction. I staggered onto Outward Bound Road not 200 yards from the jeep.

The threatening clouds passed without dropping a single snowflake, so I returned the next morning to get the Upsala Lake pack's side of the story. I picked up its tracks on an overgrown logging road that led from Birch Road to the Ontolagon River. As the road began to descend, I fastened my heels to the skis for more control. At first I slid along at walking speed, notebook in hand. I was able to record one RLU without stopping, but even as I congratulated myself on my efficiency, the slope got slightly steeper and I accelerated alarmingly. Ahead a scat and a RLU marked a place where one of the wolves had left the road. I snowplowed to a stop, narrowly avoiding the frozen scat, and recorded the sign.

The wolf had returned to the road only twenty yards ahead, so I didn't bother to follow its tracks through the bush. I was willing to risk missing a scent mark or two in order to see how the wolves had responded to trespass.

A quarter of a mile from the bottom of the hill the wolves had left the road and entered a patch of tall, widely spaced red pines. Here the tracks meandered crazily, moving from one trampled, torn-up area to another. The wolves had gone berserk, ripping brush with their teeth, scratching through the snow to send streams of leaf mold and earth five yards across the snow, urinating on everything in sight. In an area the size of three football fields there were thirty RLUs, ten scratches, a couple of SQUs, and a scat. Had there been a fight? I could find no blood, so if there had been a fight, it had probably not been serious.

Untangling the tracks would have been impossible, so I made a circle around the area to see where the Upsala Lake wolves had gone. Before I found their exit, though, I crossed the snowshoe trail I'd left the previous day when I followed the northern pack from the deer to the river. Evidently the Upsala Lake pack had encountered the fresh trail of the trespassers, but not the trespassers themselves. Already at the northern border of its turf, it had not gone after the intruders but had vented its aggression on vegetation instead. This course was probably not as satisfying as hot pursuit, but surely much safer. The Upsala Lake wolves were outnumbered almost two to one, and two of their members were pups and wouldn't be much help in a fight.

My next task was to check the deer. Hoping that a free meal would have at least in part compensated Freya's pack for the violation of its territorial rights, I started toward the deer. The shortest route to the deer carcass was back the way I came; I groaned inwardly at the thought of going back up the hill I'd just skied down, but I had little choice.

I was glad to see that the Upsala Lake wolves had found the deer. Freya's mate was missing two claws on his right forefoot (probably the result of a near miss by a steel-jawed trap), so his tracks were easy to identify. His distinctive prints, along with those of three other wolves, led to the half-consumed remains of the deer. Since Freya's signal came from nearby, I gave the carcass a wide berth and trudged back to the road.

There was a note from the local game warden under the jeep's single windshield wiper. It told me I could find a couple of road-killed deer just south of Jack Pine. Red, Gray, and Lotte hadn't had fresh meat in several days, so I picked up the road kills and hauled them to Joe's. After

161

tossing a foreleg to each wolf, I buried the rest of the deer in a convenient snowdrift.

When the wolves had eaten their fill, I attempted to capitalize on their postprandial torpor by drawing some anal-sac secretions. Red had already reduced his meal to a litter of splintered bone and was at the fence begging for attention, so I could enter the pen without arousing his proprietary ire.

As soon as I crept through the gate and hunkered he bounded over with a playful rocking-horse gait, then thrust his face into mine, knocking me against the fence. I slowly reached up to scratch his muzzle, then the matted fur behind his ears, then his belly. As I hoped, at this last endearment he threw himself onto his back, forepaws tucked against his chest like an enormous hundred-pound puppy. His tail was clamped tightly over his anus, so I brushed it gently out of the way with one hand while slipping a syringe out of my pocket with the other.

My plan was to put the wide end of the syringe sans piston into his rectum so that it lay over the duct of an anal sac. With the needle pointing out toward me, I could impale the septum of a vacutainer which would suck the secretions quickly and neatly into the airtight glass tube.

That was the plan, but as I made my move, Red arched his back, grabbed my mustache with his incisors, and tugged. I yelped with pain, threw myself upon him, and with grim determination thrust the end of the syringe into his rectum, turned it sideways to cover a duct, and jammed the vacutainer onto the needle. Red began to wriggle free, so I clamped my knees over his flanks. Reaching behind me, he grabbed the back of my leather jacket. I let him work on it as I adjusted the syringe. The vacutainer would only suck for a second or so, and I doubted Red would give me another chance. Having devoured all of the jacket he could easily reach, Red once again began to wriggle. I clamped my knees even harder. A thick brown fluid was oozing into the vacutainer, but even as I began to congratulate myself on my technique Red bucked mightily, causing the syringe to slip. A jet of acrid ooze spurted onto my face. Gagging, I jumped to my feet and groped my way to the gate, holding the syringe and my stinking hands as far away as possible. I ran to the drift where I had stashed the deer, stuck the vacutainer into the snow, and used other snow to clean my face and hands. Glancing at Red, I noted that he had run to a corner, where he sat with a hind leg raised, sniffing his rear. My attempts to make amends were in vain. He wouldn't come near me. Lotte was much easier to handle. She meekly submitted to the indignity of anal-sac expression, which proved more embarrassing than painful for both of us. Red observed the procedure from behind a tree, confirming my suspicion that his earlier attempts to interpose himself between me and the female were motivated more by jealousy over my attention than by concern for her honor.

Red's conspicuous lack of gallantry was somewhat disturbing, though, for the breeding season was only a month and a half away. Signs of possessiveness on his part would have been welcomed by all of us who hoped for a litter that spring.

The new year arrived less like a newborn babe than an errant husband; it crept in quietly on stockinged feet, shoes in hand, virtually unnoticed. After a full day of tracking I celebrated by drinking a glass of eggnog laced with rum and falling asleep in front of the fire.

Spired spruce shadows reached slowly across the snow.

Eventually one shadow's tip tickled the white wolf's nose. She woke with a snort and blinked but remained lying on her side as she arched her back, extended her legs, and brought all four feet together in a stretch. Then she rolled onto her back, wriggled sinuously, and yawned with a tiny squeak.

Her brother flicked an ear at the sound but kept his eyes shut. Still on her back, the slim young female flopped her head upside down onto the snow and swung it from side to side. There was no response from her brother. She flipped herself onto her feet, bounded to his side, and slipped her snout under his chin. Ignoring his low growl, she jerked her nose up, lifted his head, then let it drop onto the snow. His eyes stayed closed, but he rolled onto his back to let her lick his penis. She gave it a perfunctory lap, then was off at a gallop, weaving her way among the other wolves.

The old male slowly opened one eye. On the young female's next approach he growled. Both young wolves were on him in an instant, licking his face, tugging his mane, thrusting their snouts beneath his belly. He lifted a lip; the young wolves ran, this time with the male in the lead, his sister in pursuit. She gained quickly, leaped at his tail, missed, and tumbled into another sleeping wolf, which jumped to its feet, teeth flashing.

The commotion had wakened the rest of the wolves. Eyes snapped open; jaws gaped and clicked shut; legs stretched. A pure black wolf rose, ran a red tongue over ivory teeth, and shook itself from end to end, showering two others with powdery snow. The old gray male grunted as his stiff rear legs refused to budge. On his second try he made it and was immediately surrounded by the rest of the pack.

The young female escaped the melee and ran to the edge of the clearing to try a howl. It started well, but her voice broke into yips almost immediately. Her brother ran in circles, barking at the other wolves. Two of them barked back. Then the old male lifted his nose to the sky, belled his lips, and sent a low moan into the treetops. Another wolf joined in at a higher pitch, then another. Soon all six were howling, filling the forest with eerie dissonances. When they stopped, the valley rang with dying echoes, then with a reply, a wail borne on a silent wind. The wolves filed out of the clearing. The evening's hunt had begun.

I began the new year in a loathsomely wholesome manner, rising early and eating a healthy breakfast. My first and only resolution was to atone for this virtuous excess with a penance of unspeakable depravity as soon as I returned to Ann Arbor. Meanwhile, there was work to do.

I set out in the wolf project van, which was equipped with an external antenna that could be rotated from inside, allowing one to get fairly good triangulated fixes on the positions of radioed wolves without leaving the relative comfort of the driver's seat; the van was much warmer than the jeep. With its limited slip differential it was the jeep's equal on all but the very worst of roads, so I headed down the unplowed highway without trepidation.

I picked up signals from Freya as I passed Upsala Lake, but since she was close to the center of her territory, I decided to diversify my portfolio of data by following the Olympus pack, which I hadn't tracked since before Christmas.

I got a few faint beeps from the south as I passed Olympus Mountain. They were probably echoes. If the wolves

165

really were to the south, they would have to be either on the mountain, in which case the signals would have been much louder, or behind the mountain, in which case I wouldn't have picked them up at all.

Three miles east of the mountain my guess proved correct: Fresh wolf tracks emerged from Muskegon Lake Road and turned right to follow my route. It had been snowing since I left the lab, so the tracks couldn't have been more than an hour old, but a careful 360-degree scan failed to pick up any signals. I drove slowly forward, recording RLUs without leaving the warmth of the van. At the eastern edge of the Olympus territory I topped a small rise just as a momentary lull in the snowfall afforded a view of the next hill. The wolves had gone halfway up the gentle grade, milled in the center of the road, then turned back. I pulled over to the side and inspected the tracks on foot, finding more scent marks and two indentations in the snow, which looked exactly like the marks left by Red and Lotte when they rubbed on rotten meat.

I lowered my face to the snow and sniffed. Both marks had a wolfy, sweet-sour pungency, but one was much stronger than the other. I dug around with my knife until I found the carcass of a long-dead vole redolent with a pungency of its own, remarkably similar to the odor of wolf.

After the wolves had rubbed, they had gone another 100 yards, turned around, retraced their steps, and then left the road to the south. It was another case of recoil from a territorial boundary, but once again I could not tell whether the wolves had turned back because they knew where they were or because they had detected foreign sign. Almost a foot of snow had fallen that morning, and the road could be littered with scent marks of their neighbors that the Olympus wolves could smell but that I could never see.

After another radio check to assure myself that neither the Olympus pack nor its neighbors to the east were nearby, I drove back to Muskegon Lake Road. The snow was somewhat deeper there, but it was very light, and the van did not balk. I drove along slowly, luxuriating in the data I'd gathered so effortlessly. The new year was off to an excellent start—but the best was yet to come.

The wolves had joined Muskegon Lake Road after traversing a plantation of young white pines. The snow-filled air muffled the clatter of my skis as I slid them out of the van. Two hundred yards into the plantation was the carcass of a freshly killed moose. The legs and neck were gone, and so was much of the hide, but the ribs were still fully fleshed and covered with skin. They arched from a keellike spine, forming a capsized hill that could accommodate a crew of four. I traced a rosette of looping tracks as I searched for the jawbone and limb that would indicate the moose's age and health.

The morning's snowfall had obscured all tracks more than an hour old, so it was possible that the moose was dead before the wolves found it. Unreined by evidence, my imagination galloped after the wolves. Why had they left the carcass, gone to the edge of their territory, then turned back? They had not returned to the plantation, for their signals were impossible to pick up. Were they looking for trouble or simply getting some after-dinner exercise?

I left for Olympus Mountain with a couple of legs and a mandible. It took me until early afternoon to ski to the top, where my efforts were rewarded by a tight bearing on the Olympus pack. They were far to the south, and

167

from the sound of their signals they were still moving. My descent was a succession of accelerating glides, each climaxing in an ignominious face-plant, but each was a little longer than the one before. I arrived at the van frosted from head to foot but pleased with the quantity of data I'd gathered.

Hunt called that evening to see how I was doing. Certain as I was about my interpretation of the tracks that told the story of the trespass across the Ontolagon, I confined my remarks to a detailed description of the tracks themselves. Still, only after an intensive cross-examination did he finally concur with my conclusions.

The moose was the first destination of the next morning's flight. The Olympus wolves had returned for another meal. Several of them lay around the now-dismembered skeleton, chewing on bones and basking in the sun.

The Upsala Lake pack was next. As we flew over Olympus Mountain, its signal came so clearly from the south that I thought for a moment I had reversed the antenna leads, but a quick check told me they were in order. Shrugging, I pointed south. A few minutes later we crossed the Rocky River, with the signal still ahead. I found the wolves nearly ten miles out of their territory, peacefully munching a deer on the east shore of Lost Lake.

The night before, Hunt had asked me to give priority in tracking and aerial observation to trespassing wolves. With the deer population in the Lawrence National Forest at its lowest point since the wolf project had begun, it was becoming more and more difficult for wolves to obtain deer in their own territories. Some, he thought, would switch to moose or beaver, but others might have recourse to raids on their neighbors' resources. He was anxious to document any kills made on such forays. I was equally eager to examine patterns of travel and scent marking.

Since Freya and her pack were trespassing, I canceled the rest of the aerial survey and returned to Windy Point. By midmorning the jeep was rattling me past the lab on my way to Jack Pine Trail. I planned to track the trespassers for a couple of miles before and after they left their territory, in order to compare rates of scent marking in the core of their range, at its edge, and outside. I drove west along Jack Pine until I found where the pack had crossed the road. I had seen from the plane that skis would be useless in the dense timber and steep ridges they had traversed, so I strapped myself into showshoes with a sigh of resignation.

The wolf trail was as straight as any route through that country could be. It bore directly south, a narrow trench in deep snow. In the mile or so between the road and the Rocky River I found only two black, runny scats, but neither was placed on or near any target I could discern. The sun was high when I stumbled out of the bush onto an unplowed road that ran along the north shore of the river.

As though realizing they were at their southern border, the wolves had left a pair of RLUs and another drippy black scat. I followed the tracks northwest along the frozen river, barely visible through the trees to the left. After another half mile, over which they left several more scent marks, the wolves had veered abruptly to cross the river at the widest point so far, a swampy bay several hundred yards across.

In the windswept center of the bay the tracks had nearly been obliterated. Even as I watched, the few clear ones were being erased. Ahead the tracks were invisible, but I could see a white, bony scat. Puzzled, I knelt to examine it, for all the scats I'd seen that morning were black. Before rising to my feet, I glanced up and down the river; a lower point of view sometimes made it easier to spot tracks. I

169

was surprised to see a trace of tracks following the midline of the river.

I followed the tracks northwest to the edge of the bay, where a cliff had protected them from the wind. At least five wolves had traveled southeast along the river, and recently, too; even in the lee of the cliff the tracks were filling with snow. A little farther on the river bent west and narrowed. Here eight sets of tracks showed clearly. The Lost Lake pack, Freya's unradioed southern neighbors, had eight wolves. They must have left these tracks; Freya's pack could have only if it had traveled down from Upsala Lake, made two trips down the river, traveled another eight miles to Lost Lake, then killed and eaten a deer, all within twenty-four hours. Such a program was well within its physical capabilities but was unlikely. Had the Lost Lake pack come down the river after Freya had crossed? These tracks looked fresher than Freya's, especially near the white scat, but a larger number of wolves might well have left a deeper, longer-lasting trail.

With the sun behind me as I returned to the scat, I could see that two sets of the eight had peeled off to follow the intruders' trail to the southern shore. I followed suit. The two newer sets of tracks joined those of Freya's pack and took the same route to a small cliff. This obstacle had not deterred the trespassers, but the Lost Lake wolves had turned back. I scrambled up the cliff.

I followed Freya only far enough to assure myself that she had resumed her freeway-straight southerly heading. I then returned to the river to see what the Lost Lake wolves had done. The tracks of the two that had peeled off rejoined the trail left by the others. All eight sets then continued down the river. I followed them as far as Route 3, another four miles, finding six more white, bony scats and five RLUs. Apart from the brief and abortive pursuit, the Lost Lake pack's only response to a recent trespass had been a dramatic rise in its rate of scent marking. Whatever had caused these wolves to patrol their northern border, it was evidently not a search for "trouble."

Looking for trouble or not, one of the wolves had found it, in the form of thin ice. I had to chuckle at the cartoonlike clarity of the sign: A set of tracks led to a wolf-sized hole in the ice. There was a place on the rim of the hole where the wolf had scratched the snow away as it clawed its way out, and a few yards farther on a spray of tiny holes in the snow showed where it had shaken itself off. With its thick, waterproof fur it had probably found the dunking a minor inconvenience, but I shuddered as I glanced at the black water rushing beneath the hole.

I made it to Route 3 at dusk and walked north along the shoulder. A vehicle roared around a turn behind me and began to slow even before I had a chance to raise a thumb. I was back at the lodge in time to join Bert for dinner.

After a day on snowshoes I was too tired to accept Bert's invitation to join him for a night of howling. It was just as well, for he was back in less than two hours. "You'll never guess where the Olympus pack is," he commented, warming his hands over the stove.

"They're at the Jolly Trapper having beers and shots."

"Nope. They're south of Route 3 near Norman Lake, moving south. I didn't want to interfere with a possible trespass, so I came right back. And Freya is heading back north."

"It's a good thing. It's turning into a wolf convention down there. I didn't think there were that many deer down that way."

"Looks as if the wolves do, though."
Bert and I agreed to go tracking the next day.

The morning sky was overcast—not good for tracking. It took us several trips up and down Route 3 before we found where the wolves had crossed. We could get no signals there, so we drove back to the junction with Route 4 and turned south. We found the tracks, this time with the aid of several ravens perched on trees over a fresh kill, not twenty yards from the road. "Probably hit by a car," Bert surmised. I grunted, but after six wolves had had their fill, there wasn't enough of the deer left to tell how it had died. The wolves had moved south without leaving any beds we could find. I sent Bert backtracking to the north while I followed them south.

I had been on the trail only about fifteen minutes when I heard the unmistakable "rroooo" of one of Bert's 100-decibel howls. I was being summoned. The wolf trail had run more or less parallel to the road, so it took me only a few minutes to snowshoe out. I stood in the road and waved until Bert spotted me and drove up in the jeep.

Bert's customary phlegmatic calm was not in evidence. He had found two trails, one headed south, the other north, gradually diverging from each other. Realizing that a return to Olympus territory by a route different from that used on the trip south would suggest some sense of spatial relationships or at least of direction, Bert followed the trail that led north to see if it continued to diverge from the other. Almost immediately he had found blood. A few minutes later he had come across a wolf bed on a snow-covered boulder. The bed was soaked with blood. It was too early for a female to be coming into heat, so one of the wolves must have been injured.

We planned our next moves. The previous night Bert had picked up the Olympus pack's signals a little farther south, near the Dana Mining Company's railroad tracks. Since whatever had caused the trespassers to retreat was likely to have occurred at the southernmost point of their route, we decided to drive a little south of the railroad and try to pick up the trail there.

"Let's go in together," I suggested. "When we find the trail, you can go one way, I the other."

"Fine. But this time you backtrack. Trying to imagine everything backwards gives me a headache."

We did not have to go far to find the trail. Evidently the pack had followed the highway but kept to the woods, not a bad strategy for travel in unfamiliar and unfriendly country. The wolves had fanned out, so rather than split up, as we had planned, Bert and I both moved in the direction taken by the wolves, retracing our steps when necessary to follow every set of tracks. Within half an hour my sketch of the tracks looked like a schematic diagram of a plate of spaghetti.

The tracks led us down a series of natural embankments toward a swamp. From the edge of the last of these benches we could see a bowl, six or seven yards across, which had been trampled into the snow. The surrounding vegetation had been ravaged: limbs bent and broken; a willow sapling chewed almost in half; fragments of leaves and bark everywhere. We circled for a better view before marking the area with our own tracks. A second trampled bowl appeared, just beyond the first. A wolf lay in the center. We froze.

The wolf did not move; it was lying on its side, facing away from us, so it could have been asleep. I doubted it, for we had made no attempt to be silent as we followed

173

the tangle of tracks. Bert took a few pictures, and then I jumped down into the first bowl. The wolf did not respond. I walked slowly over to the next bowl, more certain at every step that the animal was dead. Nevertheless, I had one hand on my knife while I reached gingerly with the other to touch the wolf's haunch. Startled by a human, it might snap defensively rather than bolt. My anxiety was unfounded. The wolf was cold and stiff.

Sheepishly I looked back at Bert. As I might have guessed, he was observing my progress through the lens of his camera, ready to record my encounter with the wolf in the unlikely event it should prove worthy of recording. He looked a little disappointed as he joined me in the bowl to shoot a few more pictures before we examined the wolf. I made a quick sketch as he did so, then turned the wolf over. The side on which it had been lying was matted with frozen blood. There were no bullet holes, and the ribs and legs felt intact, so it was unlikely he had been shot or hit by a car.

Bert and I quickly ran through the list of possible killers. Bears were sleeping, and besides another wolf, the only local nonhuman that could conceivably kill a wolf was a lynx. We would have to search the area with great care, for especially in deep, powdery snow, the tracks of a lynx would be difficult to distinguish from those of wolves.

We got to work quickly, for the darkness overhead told us that snow might fall at any moment. We each swept a wide semicircle that would bring us back to the road by sundown. My first sweep was not wide enough. I kept coming across untraceable tangles of wolf tracks that told me only that there had been a lot of running and very little scent marking. I backtracked and made a much wider sweep, hoping to find the trail of a pack traveling single file toward or away from the dead wolf. Such a trail would give me some idea where the other pack had come from. Eventually I found such a trail heading directly toward the scene of the crime from the north, where the Lost Lake pack had been the day before. Several single trails left the swamp, all headed generally north. I followed each one until I found a print clear enough to show claws, which meant it was left by a wolf, not by a lynx.

I hauled the dead wolf out on my shoulders and placed it in the jeep. Bert had located the tracks of the Olympus pack. It had started back along the same route it came south on but had veered from time to time, allowing him to confirm that one of the wolves had been wounded after coming south and before returning to the north. I suggested we head for home and try to reconstruct what had happened as we drove.

Hunt was at the lab. Seated at the kitchen table, he was going over the flight sheets of the previous week. He had come up early because the end of February would be devoted to last-minute preparations for a reintroduction of wolves to an adjacent state. After examining the wolf carcass, he had us plot on a single map all the sign we'd found. What emerged was unmistakably an encounter between the Olympus and Lost Lake packs in which a wolf had been killed. The victim was probably a member of the Lost Lake pack because there was no male wolf of its age in the Olympus pack. For news of the fate of the injured Olympus wolf, we would have to wait until the next morning's flight.

Bert accompanied Hunt on the flight while I tracked the Olympus pack's return to its territory. The divergence between its routes coming and going continued to widen.

Like the trespassers into Freya's territory who had killed the deer on Christmas Day, the wolves had returned not by retracing the trail they had already broken but by taking a shorter, more direct route. Since both trespassing packs were traveling in terra incognita, neither rote learning nor scent-trail following was a plausible explanation. What remained was some sort of sense of direction or of spatial relationships. Trespasses were perfect natural experiments in spatial knowledge; it was tragic that they were so dangerous for the wolves involved. Finding myself hoping for more, I was ashamed that my personal concern for the welfare of the radioed packs could be so easily challenged by professional curiosity about the course of future trespasses.

The guilt generated by this conflict was partially assuaged by the news that Hunt and Bert not only had found all six members of the Olympus pack together on their own turf but had been unable to tell from the air which wolf had been hurt. Its injury, then, must have been slight.

It was several weeks before I was forced to confront the issue again. As Hunt brought us in on the signal of wolf Akbar of the Mogul Lake pack, I remarked that the day before I had got his signal and that of Behti, another radioed wolf in the pack, in that same location, a couple of miles east of their territory. Hunt switched to Behti's frequency, then back to Akbar's. His brow rippled with concern as he passed the headphones back to me.

"See if the signal seems to come from *exactly* the same place," he said.

I listened carefully. As far as I could tell, it did.

"Sam, can you land near the east shore?" Hunt asked.

The reply was a low pass over the ice and an affirmative nod.

"Put us down as close as you can to where we've been circling," Hunt instructed. Then, turning to me, he explained, "Ordinarily I'd wait one more day before going in. A signal coming from exactly the same place for three days almost always means a slipped collar or a dead wolf. But I couldn't pick up Behti's signal, and with Akbar way out of his territory I think we'd better go in."

Sam taxied almost to the shore, turned into the wind, and cut the switches, leaving a silence that the whirring of the gyrocompass, the static on the radio, and the whispering wind could not begin to fill. Our voices sounded tinny and false, as though we were speaking over tiny transistor radios. Hunt climbed out. I passed him the portable antenna and two pairs of snowshoes, then climbed down.

"We should be back in an hour or so," said Hunt as he lashed himself into his bear-paws.

"I'm not going anywhere," replied Sam, demonstrating the solidity of his intention by sliding his seat back in preparation for a nap.

I took a bearing on Akbar's signal. Hunt, noting the direction the antenna was pointed, led the way up a wide, shallow drainage. I soon tired of staring at his back, so I took the lead, weaving through the trees with the antenna held before me like a crucifix. When we reached the top of the first ridge, I took another bearing. The signal came from the right. Soon the signal came in loud with the gain all the way down. I unplugged the antenna and could still hear the beeps. "He's right around here someplace," I said, letting Hunt lead the way again. He moved ahead cautiously, stopping to look around after every step. Suddenly he halted and motioned me to join him.

Akbar lay on his side, tongue lolling. An inch of fresh

snow covered most of his body, but it could not conceal the blood on his chest. I clicked a couple of pictures before Hunt moved in.

"Nothing but wolf tracks around," Hunt muttered. "Some under the new snow, some on top of it."

"The killer returns to the scene of the crime," I suggested. Hunt did not reply. The evidence was circumstantial but damning. Akbar had been killed by wolves, probably the residents of the territory in which he and his pack had been trespassing.

"Too bad we don't have a collar in the pack that lives here," Hunt said. "Why don't you start dragging him out of here while I make a quick check for sign?"

I put a nylon line around the wolf's neck and began to drag the corpse behind me. Whenever the going got too rough or I tired of the strain, I carried Akbar across my shoulders. His check complete, Hunt overtook me quickly and offered to help with the wolf. "What are graduate students for anyway?" I replied, and kept dragging.

Akbar and I shared the back seat as we flew a search pattern in the hope of spotting the resident pack. Hunt, of course, was the first to see it, about a mile from where we'd found the victim. Three wolves lay asleep on a sunny ledge overlooking a lake, so peaceful that it was almost impossible to believe that they were responsible for the bloody carcass beside me.

There was no easy way to turn off Akbar's collar, and with its signal reverberating in the metal cabin, further radio tracking would be nearly impossible. Somehow Hunt managed to find the rest of Akbar's pack, asleep on the shore of a small lake, well within their territory, but then it was time to head for home.

Hunt was anxious to get Akbar's carcass and that of the

Lost Lake wolf back to Northton for autopsy. There was no doubt about the fact that they had been killed by other wolves, but he wanted to have the details recorded officially. An hour after we had landed he was on his way with only the dead wolves for company.

11

Transplants

The lodge throbbed with the silence that always followed Hunt's departure. Against the sound of the flames flickering in the hearth and the scratching of my pen, the hiss and snap of the notebook pages were like tiny fireworks.

The ring of the telephone jerked me to my feet. It was Hunt calling from Northton. Thomas Mains, the trapper who provided us with bait, urine, and advice, had caught several members of a pack that was to be transplanted to safer climes. Before things went any further, we had to verify that they were indeed members of the same pack. The idea was to establish a stable breeding unit; members of the same pack will be more likely to stick together in unfamiliar terrain. Besides, they can hunt more efficiently together than separately. Could I get up to Mains's place near the Canadian border and see if they were members of the same pack?

Early the next morning I drove to the trapper's home. He pulled in behind me as I parked. His hair was white and crewcut, his face square and weathered. Shaking hands with Mains was like putting my hand into one of his traps, but I managed to escape without wincing. He immediately made it clear that he thought I was on a fool's errand. "They're from the same pack, all right. Caught 'em all within a mile of each other."

He had placed the wolves in separate but adjacent cages. I had hoped that they would show signs of affection that would make introductions unnecessary, but like most recently trapped wild animals, they ignored each other and everything else. Nor was there any striking similarity in their pelage: One was brown and black, another brindled and smoky, two others gray.

Clearly, tact was required. To have caught any four wolves within as many weeks, whether they were from the same pack or not, was an accomplishment beyond the capability of most wolf trappers. I resorted to the diplomat's standby and passed the buck. "Well, if you say they're from the same pack, that's good enough for me. But you know how Doc Hunt is—everything's got to be double-checked. He sent me all the way up here to do it, and if it's all right with you, I'd like to put a couple of 'em together, so we can say we did."

Mains grunted a grudging acknowledgment, then stalked off to get a pair of pliers to open the fence between the cages. By the time he returned, I'd wrapped my leather jacket around my left forearm and unlatched the cage containing the smallest of the wolves. As I crawled through the gate, it cowered in the corner, head tucked beneath its tail. I undid the fence, pulled it up, and backed out. Neither of the wolves moved. I walked away, then crept back to a well-concealed vantage point to watch.

After about fifteen minutes the small female the cage of which I'd entered got up, sniffed the fence where I'd

181

touched it, and slid into the cage with the other wolf, which Mains had identified as an older female. The larger female snapped twice but did not growl. We could hear her jaws click shut each time. Undaunted, the small female pawed the other's back, sniffed her face, and lay down beside her. She then began to snuffle the older wolf's mane. Snuffling is an expression of affiliation seen only among pack members that are especially intimate. The larger wolf's lips relaxed, her eyes softened, and she laid her chin on her forepaws. After five minutes it appeared they both were asleep.

Mains left me to my own devices. Turning my attention to the males, I noted that they lay side by side, separated only by the mesh between their cages. Mains's assertion that he'd trapped in only one pack was looking more and more credible. I walked slowly to the cage adjacent to the one in which both females still lay peacefully. If only I could get one of the males to interact with them, I'd be able to confirm Mains's contention.

I crawled into the empty cage that separated the females from the males, hoping that if I unhooked a section of fence, one of the females might approach the nearer male. He, however, had other plans. I had no sooner slipped through the gate than he hurled himself at the fence with such force that I was knocked down. Fear for my own safety was quickly supplanted by concern for his, for though the chain links held firm, he shook them so furiously that his lips and gums began to bleed. I decided that since Mains had been right so far, it was unnecessary for me to test his judgment further.

I hurried back to the warmth of the house and informed him that the formalities were over. He was unimpressed by my confirmation of what he had known all along but was courteous enough to keep his I-told-you-sos to himself. I used his phone to report to Hunt, who received my report with audible relief. He went on to explain that he would need someone to help him train transplant researchers in tracking and radio location. Would I be able to spare a few days from my tracking to help out? I replied enthusiastically that I would, for the transplant would provide a unique opportunity to observe the movements of wolves in totally unfamiliar terrain. Any differences between their movements and those of wolves in their own territories might provide some indication of how important memory and scent marks were.

I arrived at Hunt's home in Lester, a suburb of Northton, a few days later. We left immediately for the release. Hunt explained that the transplant, which had already assumed the administrative proportions of the Normandy invasion, had acquired some of its secrecy as well. The exact place and time of the release were known only to Hunt, Dave Williard, who directed the release end of the operation, and Ray Moore, a graduate student whose master's thesis would be based on the results of the transplant.

Arriving at Williard's home near the Lake Superior shore, we were met at the door by a dark-haired, intense man in his middle twenties, who introduced himself as Ray Moore and quickly ushered us into the den, where Williard sat next to an old-fashioned console radio, listening intently.

"Uh-oh," said Hunt.

I understood his dismay. The voice on the radio was that of Hunt's Moriarty, an articulate demagogue who had for years harangued the people of Northton with descriptions of an elaborate international conspiracy involving wolves, drugs, communism, and the Federal Reserve System. By allowing the ravenous wolf population to explode, the dope-peddling Communists who control the Federal Reserve Board were killing all the deer in America, forcing deer hunters, the country's last true patriots, to rely on meat from commercial sources, which were, of course, owned and controlled by those very Commies in pin-striped suits so often seen in schoolyards and at the Fed. This was bound to appeal to some residents around the release site, for many of whom deer hunting was not a sport but an economic necessity.

Over breakfast the next morning Hunt and Williard worked over the last-minute details of the release. The wolves were already in a holding pen on the grounds of the Thule Mountain Club, a huge private hunting reserve. With the guns of a large portion of the local able-bodied male population fully loaded, the release would be conducted so as to maximize the wolves' chances of survival. It would take place at dusk so that if the location were somehow leaked, the wolves would have twelve hours of darkness to penetrate the cordon of red-eyed patriots that might surround them.

The murmur of conversation was interrupted by a tattoo of snaps and clicks. For an instant I imagined hundreds of safety catches clicking off, then a barrage of shotgun pellets on the roof. Williard hid his face in his palms.

"Rain," he said. "It's raining."

In my relief it took me a moment to realize why he was upset. A mid-March rain would freeze on contact, compacting the snow, coating every surface with rime. By late afternoon, as the temperature dropped, the hunting reserve would be one huge skating rink. The deer, no longer confined to their yards by deep snow, would begin to disperse. The wolves, too, would find travel much easier and might well wander far from the safety of the area around the release site before they settled down.

184

There was an additional difficulty: On the icy surface that was sure to ensue, wolves would leave no tracks. Already uncertain about my ability to teach skills I myself was still acquiring, I could see only disaster ahead.

There was no hope of postponement. Enormous bureaucratic flywheels had been set in motion: Observers from the State Game and Wildlife Service had flown in the previous night, and a press conference had been scheduled for that evening. The countdown had begun.

Ours was the only vehicle on the ice-coated highway as we entered the forest wilderness to the north of Tusconing. The Thule Mountains were a concentration camp for deer. Everywhere I looked, emaciated whitetails stood in small groups, scratching at the frozen snow in pitiful attempts to find something to eat. There was no underbrush whatsoever; the forest was a marmoreal deer park, where deer grazed on ice. The Regional Department of Natural Resources estimates that deer in the Thule Mountains consume ninety-five percent of available browse by the end of each winter. That winter, in the Thule Mountains, that estimate was wildly optimistic. The deer had consumed everything edible below the height the largest ones could reach while rearing on hind legs.

I slowed as we passed a small herd on the shoulder. A large deer reared to reach the overhanging branches of a fir just beyond its reach. Failing, it hopped twice on its hind legs, then fell onto its side and lay twitching on the icy snow. I glanced at Hunt. He stared straight ahead, and a muscle twitched in his jaw.

The plight of the Thule Mountain whitetail was the inevitable consequence of a political system that allowed timber companies to create a habitat in which deer numbers soared. When the habitat changed through processes of growth and succession, in this area, as in other cases,

185

the deer population had to decline. Since in this area the same anthropocentric ideology that prescribed extermination of the deer's natural predators also proscribed the killing of innocent does, the decline would be by starvation, not by hunting. The transplant was one small victory over this ideology, but four wolves would make only a small dent in the huge deer herds of the Thule Mountains.

From the point of view of the transplanted wolves, of course, the Thule Mountains were paradise, the door of their pen a canine version of the pearly gates. As we arrived at the enclosure, a group of twenty deer munched bare alder stems not thirty yards away. Two of the wolves watched them intently, while the other two chewed the remains of one of the deer's road-killed relatives. The wolves' prospects for survival looked a little better than they had that morning. These deer had obviously never seen a wolf.

The rain had halted, and under clearing but still cloudy skies the temperature was dropping. Hunt checked the signals from the wolves' radio collars. He muttered a mild oath as he twiddled the tuning knob on the receiver. "Female One's radio has gone out," he announced, shutting the lid with a snap. "I don't want her groggy this evening when we let them go, so we'll have to handle her without drugs." He pulled the pack containing the radio-collaring gear from the truck.

As we walked to the pen, Williard and Moore pulled up. While I distracted the wolves, Moore guarded the gate and Hunt and Williard tackled the small female. Holding her in a headlock, Hunt hauled her out, while Williard held her furiously jerking hind legs. The little wolf twisted and grabbed Hunt's left hand between her jaws. I ran to assist. He instructed me to tie her legs before attempting to release his hand. With all four legs lashed together and Williard holding her down, the wolf was immobilized. Moore and I pried her jaws open. Hunt yanked his hand free and gingerly pulled off his buckskin glove, working one finger at a time. His palm bore a perfect impression of the wolf's upper teeth.

"As you can see," he explained in professional tones, "this wolf is quite young. The cusps of the carnassials are still sharp." He illustrated this comment by pointing to a pair of deep gashes in the web between thumb and forefinger. "Moreover, the lateral incisors have not yet assumed the chiseled edge characteristic of the older wolf." He indicated a couple of wide, rectangular punctures in the fleshy ridge below his little finger. "Fortunately the canines missed." He showed us two deep slots in the unbroken skin on the edge of his hand. Before we could applaud this display of professional aplomb, Hunt was back at work, measuring the wolf's neck for the collar.

The transmitter passed its range test at sunset; I was able to pick up its signal more than a mile down the road. Hunt untied the little female's feet, unwrapped her muzzle, and hastily backed away. She lay motionless for a moment, the eye we could see darting from us to the pen, then to the woods, and back to us. She scrambled to her feet. Then, with her claws rattling on the frozen snow, she scampered for the trees.

Williard and Moore opened the gate, but the other wolves cowered in a corner, showing no inclination to leave. It was not until after dark that the next wolf left. We took turns watching the wolves through a light-amplifying (starlight) scope from a shed fifty yards away. The skies had cleared, and in the twinkling green field of the scope

187

the wolves could be seen clearly. They glanced nervously at the open gate. Eventually one of them stuck its head out but immediately jumped back as though startled to find an opening.

At length the large male sniffed his way to the gate, then carefully ran his nose around the edge of the opening, lingering at every place where one of us had touched it. He sprang through without warning, then, with his nose to the snow, followed the route taken by Female One. A few seconds later another wolf bolted, taking the same course. The remaining wolf, however, was reluctant to leave the enclosure. He lay in a corner, snuggled between the fence and the carcass of a road-killed deer.

After what seemed like an hour but could have been only a few minutes, Hunt recommended that we chase him out. By pounding on the posts with hammers, shaking the fence, and barking like cowboys on a cattle drive, we eventually shooed him through the gate. He put his nose to the ground and trotted after the others. There were four more wolves in the state.

A meeting with Division of Natural Resources and Game and Wildlife officials, for which Hunt, Williard, and Moore were already late, left them no time to savor the event. They were sprinting for Williard's car as soon as the last wolf was out of sight. I remained, for I was to meet the students I would train at the enclosure early the next morning. I settled into the roomy rear of the truck and by flashlight scribbled an account of the release. I sipped the last of my brandy and from time to time clicked on the receiver. Each time the signals of the immigrant wolves were weaker.

My students woke me by tapping gently on the side of the truck. After exchanging introductions and views on the combination of waxes best suited for skiing on solid ice, we set off, double-poling on the nearly frictionless surface. The signals of two of the wolves came from the southwest, so we had a general idea which way to head, but as I feared, the wolves had left no tracks.

I suggested that we get a little practice in radio tracking before fanning out to look for scent marks. As I assembled the antenna, the drone of a distant plane developed the periodic Doppler shift that told me it was circling. Hunt and Moore had located the wolves. We climbed a small hill and were able to see the circling airplane. I passed the receiver, earphones, and antenna to one of the students. Three of the signals came from the direction of the plane, but we could not pick up the beeps from Female One. She had evidently not yet joined the others.

As we were to learn later that afternoon when we met with Hunt and Moore, she not only had not joined the others but was more than six miles to the south. It was no wonder we'd been unable to pick up her signal. By that time I'd taught the new researchers everything I knew about radio tracking from the ground, so they left with Hunt for a press conference in Northton. With the release of the wolves, Hunt had completed a project that had begun more than three years before.

Hunt arrived at Ontolagon a week later, bearing news of the transplanted wolves and some news of his own, in the form of a large female wolf sleeping peacefully on the back seat of his car. He explained the sleeping wolf first. He'd been trying for years to get permission to live-trap and transplant wolves that preyed on cattle in north-central ranch land. With the success of the transplant operation he'd finally gotten it. Although he couldn't guarantee this wolf a utopia like the Thule Mountains, its fate was sure to be better than that which usually awaits depredating wolves.

While Milo prepared a radio collar, Hunt brought us up to date on the relocated wolves. After a few days of wandering three of them (all but Female One) had traveled west of the release site. Female One had headed in the opposite direction. All had left the core of wilderness in which it had been hoped they would settle, but all were still alive. Hunt hoped our own transplant would go as well. He didn't want to release a groggy wolf into unfamiliar country, so we'd let her go in the morning. After putting the still-unconscious wolf in a cage, he took us inside to show us his latest map of local wolf territories. There was a small zone well populated with deer but unoccupied by wolves to the northeast of the Olympus territory. We would release her there.

Everyone who worked at the lab found an excuse to come along; both the jeep and the van were packed with people, cameras, daypacks, a six-pack or two, and the wolf, now ear-tagged and known informally as Muff. We drove east on Jack Pine Trail through the Olympus territory to the center of the unoccupied zone. After ascertaining that the wolf was fully awake, and her radio broadcasting at full power, Hunt set up his movie camera on top of the van. Bert and I took to the brush on opposite sides of the road, hoping to get a picture of the wolf running toward us; by then we both had plenty of pictures of wildlife running away.

After a flurry of activity we were ready for anything the wolf might do, with one exception: We all knew that as a rule wild wolves will do anything to avoid contact with humans, so no one considered even for a moment the possibility that she might attack. No one but I, that is, for as Milo got ready to drop the gate, I realized that someone who stood between a wolf and its escape route might well be the unfortunate exception that proved the rule.

Hunt started his camera as Milo released the latch and jumped back. The wolf sat still, only her eyes moving. Hunt stopped the camera while Milo packed a snowball and tossed it lightly at the cage. The wolf was out of the cage faster than my lens could follow. She became a blur until I realized I was refocusing in the wrong direction; I needed to focus closer, not farther away. As I twisted my lens, she became a wolf again, running straight at me. I shot, refocused, and shot again. Suddenly she filled the frame, her nose a blur. My camera could focus no closer. I stood up quickly and kept on shooting. With my eye to the camera I couldn't tell how close she came, but my lens could focus down to about six feet. One of my last shots was filled with the blurred image of her tail.

For the next few days Muff stayed within a mile of the release site, then gradually moved to the northwest, on a bearing that led to her former range. The route taken by the other transplants was also in the general direction of their home, but they were turned back by the lake. As we learned from Williard later that week, after encountering the lake, they had moved southwest, then northwest again, traversing the base of the Cohowah Peninsula in what was beginning to look like a serious attempt to return to their home.

For the next few weeks, as I trudged after wolves through increasingly soggy snow, I wondered how Muff and the other transplants had known which way to go. They had been transported in vehicles that afforded them no view of landmarks, sky, or passing scenery. As I followed one of Freya's compass-straight routes through deep forest, I wondered if wolves might be able to navigate like birds, using the sun, stars, or even the earth's magnetic field. I hoped not—I was supposed to be eliminating hypotheses, not generating new ones.

Muff never traveled far enough to demonstrate homing. After her brief excursion to the northwest she returned to the area where she'd been released. Meanwhile, the wandering pack of transplants had moved back toward the deer-infested forests of the Thule Mountains. There was more good news from our own study areas: In spite of the paucity of deer, Freya was denning up.

12
Survival

The forest smelled like denning time, of wet fur and damp earth, moist, musty, and dank. It sounded like denning time, too; there were new songs in the treetops and loud snaps from the lakes. The thawing ice was still firm enough for travel, but Freya did not hunt. When her mate tried to rouse her by pawing her protruding ribs, the sound was a hollow thump. She raised her head but could not reach his face. Her head fell limply onto the soggy snow.

Frey licked his mate's muzzle, then stepped back. His quiet "woof" brought the yearlings bounding. They slowed as they approached him, then in turn touched his muzzle with theirs, coming from below awkwardly but with great care; though they were still lean and long-legged, they were almost as tall as their sire. Freya raised her head to watch them trot out onto the lake, then lay back and fell into a troubled sleep.

When the wolves returned, the sun was high and warm. Frey dropped a rabbit in front of Freya's jaws and backed away. Ordinarily she would have swallowed it in a couple *of gulps, but this time she could barely get it down. By the time she finished, her mate and pups were gone again. She could hear the snow crunching as they made their way up the ridge.*

Revived by her meal, she rose and slowly made her way to the old den. The entrance had caved in, but the earth was soft. She was not too weak to dig; she scratched away until she was exhausted, lay on her side, panting until she caught her breath, then went back to work, hurling the dirt between her hind legs until the entrance was clear. The pups returned at dusk but brought no food. Her mate did not come back until dawn, and he, too, had nothing to offer. When she licked the corners of his mouth, his belly heaved, but all that came was a watery liquid. She lapped it avidly.

The night was cold, but the snow had long since melted from the area around the mouth of the den. Freya and her mate huddled there as the sun moved higher, dozing until they were wakened by a roar that circled in the sky.

The Upsala Lake pack was hard to see against the south-facing slope, where snow lay only in patches, but the mound of fresh earth showed me where to look. Nevertheless, it was only when three of them got to their feet that I was sure I was looking at wolves, not rocks. The fourth wolflike form did not move.

"Let's get out of here," I said to Sam. "She's digging out the den—there's no point in disturbing her any more than we already have."

My words reflected more than my avuncular concern for Freya and her pack, for this year deer were scarcer than ever before. There were plenty of moose, but a healthy moose could stand off a pack of only four wolves almost indefinitely. A litter this year would provide the numbers the pack would need later on, when being able to kill moose might make the difference between survival and starvation.

None of the other radioed packs were traveling near the boundaries of their territories, so we circled them only long enough to plot their locations. As the end of my second winter on the wolf project approached, I was concentrating on packs that were likely to find the spoor of other packs. I had often followed the tracks of wolves that had encountered foreign scent marks, but I had yet to observe such an encounter directly.

After several more flights I still had not seen the event that was the focus of my research. It hardly seemed fair —Bert had heard wolves howling hundreds of times; why couldn't I see a wolf react to a foreign scent mark just once? Eventually I was forced to conclude that I'd have to follow Bert's example; he'd heard so many howls because he produced howls of his own. If I were to see what I wanted, I'd have to arrange the encounter myself, and there was only one way to do this without leaving odors of my own: I'd have to drop scent marks from an airplane.

The first step was to collect some urine. I had learned that any attempt to handle Lotte with Red in the same pen would turn into a tag-team match, so I first shooed him into the other pen. Ordinarily Lotte would have been ready for a romp, but she spotted the beaker in my hand and shied away, so I sat quietly in a corner until curiosity and affection got the better of her. Then, with a combination of murmured endearments, delicate scratches, and gentle judo, I soon had her on her back, writhing sensuously with tongue lolling. I stroked her belly, meanwhile slipping the beaker into position. Gradually I

195

increased the pressure on her lower abdomen. As the realization dawned that I was not merely playing, Lotte yelped and tried to get to her feet. I threw myself on top of her and let her munch on the already well-chewed hem of my leather jacket while I applied even greater pressure. It was probably alarm, not my manipulation, that produced the result I was after, but in any case I was rewarded with a golden stream. Within seconds I had enough for several scent marks. I got to my feet and made my escape, holding the beaker of precious liquid high above my head as she leaped again and again to thwart the theft. Red had watched the whole operation. When I went to the fence to give him a scratch, he turned away as if in disgust.

Now that I had the payload, I needed a delivery system. The most logical vehicle would be a chunk of snow, but even if a snowball did not disintegrate in the slipstream, its ballistics would be hard to predict. I opted for a device that though artificial, ought to be highly reliable: the water balloon. The very conditions that rendered the snow unsuitable for tracking made it perfect for dropping balloons; the afternoon thaw and evening freeze had created a hard, icy surface on which balloons were certain to burst.

Or so I thought. Several flights went by without an opportunity for a drop; we had to catch a pack moving on a predictable course, so we could avoid disturbing them. Then, late one morning, we found the Trojan Lake pack moving single file along the still-frozen Michigas River. We watched long enough to be fairly sure that the wolves would stay on the river, then made a pass at treetop level about half a mile ahead of them. At Sam's command I popped the window, and when he shouted, "Now!" I dropped the balloon. We banked and flew back to the wolves, which were still coming up the river. Our next circle took us over the balloon. Though dropped onto solid ice from a height of sixty feet at a speed of 100 miles an hour, it had failed to burst. The bright yellow sphere lay insolently on the ice as the pack paced by, never giving it a glance.

"That'll never happen again in a million years," said Sam.

"Right, but just the same let's use a little more altitude on the next one."

Sam nodded, but the next day two urine balloons, the second inflated dangerously close to bursting, also proved to be duds. I would have to risk the dubious integrity and uncertain trajectory of natural scent marks. I spent the afternoon on skis tracking Frey. By dusk I'd collected a veritable arsenal: two juicy scats and four large hunks of yellow snow. I stored them all in a styrofoam cooler above a layer of ice to keep them from melting.

The next morning we flew under a cloudy ceiling, which descended steadily as we flew toward the first pack. "Much lower, and we'll have to turn back," said Sam. He repeated for the Nth time the adage about the scarcity of old, bold pilots.

There was just enough light to see the web of frozen lakes and streams through shreds of gray vapor. The altitude, the hour, and the clouds combined to create a dreamlike mood, but occasional air pockets with their sudden moments of free fall were reminders that however magical the scene, we were still subject to the laws of physics, universal gravitation included.

We followed a signal to the Razor River, where a pack of four moved briskly between high cliffs. It was a perfect opportunity for a drop. The first clump of snow disintegrated as soon as I released it; the second got caught in a

197

crosswind and landed in the trees. By the time we returned for our next run, the wolves had disappeared.

The conditions for the next drop were less favorable, but with the ceiling continuing to fall and my ordnance beginning to melt, I decided to risk it. A pack of three were traveling east near the center of Winipeg Lake. Their route had been straight so far, so we dropped a chunk of yellow snow half a mile ahead of them and climbed to watch their reaction. The lead wolf walked right up to it, sniffed it with ears and tail down. He then sniffed the surrounding snow as though puzzled by the absence of tracks. He sniffed the urine again, then rubbed and rolled on it. The two other wolves stood watching, their heads cocked to the side.

"Why do they roll in stuff like that?" asked Sam.

"I don't know for sure, but Kleiman claims that wolves rub in novel odors to make them more familiar and hence less threatening. That theory never made much sense to me until now; that guy had his ears and tail down as though he were plenty worried. Look at him now." The wolf was back in the lead, tail flagging as he made for the shore.

A few days later I was able to drop a scat in front of the mate and pups of Akba, who'd been killed while trespassing. As might have been expected, their reaction was dramatic. As soon as the lead wolf got within smelling range, she slowed down, then made a sharp right turn and ran from the river into the trees. We could see her there, so we located another pack and returned to find her two miles away, still traveling fast. "I guess she doesn't like the smell any more than I do," said Sam.

We circled until the wolves were once again lost from view, then flew off on a tangent to Olympus Mountain, where the Olympus wolves were hanging around their den. In spite of the shortage of deer in their territory, they seemed to be doing well. They all were sprawled in the sun atop the huge granite block that was the roof of the den. I guessed that they might be getting a moose now and then.

I had deliberately saved Freya for last. I knew she'd be at her den, and so she was, alone as usual, for the signals of her packmates came from far away. I soon realized, however, that she'd be impossible to spot, for her signal came from the trees below the den's mouth. I stowed the receiver and signaled Sam to take us home.

At the lab I found a letter from my dissertation committee, pestering me for a report on my progress. My problem was that I had no progress to report. New questions had continued to appear faster than I could answer the old ones. Freya and her mate did make shortcuts and detours, which suggested that they might be able to use mental maps. On the other hand, the movements of the wandering transplants raised the possibility that wolves could home like pigeons. I'd have to eliminate that possibility before I could conclude that cognitive maps were important determinants of wolf travel.

I also had to eliminate the even simpler possibility that wolves simply followed their own odor trails around as rats are known to do. In order to discount that possibility, I had to know how long scent marks could last before their odor became too faint for a wolf to detect them. At the end of April, when tracking had become futile, I decided it was time for a different kind of research.

Hunt supplied me with some urine from captive wolves in Northton, so I was able to begin almost immediately. By presenting urine in what was by then the WOLF Mark

V, I arrived at an estimate in only two weeks. It appeared that Red and Lotte could detect samples of urine applied to twigs, rocks, bark, and blocks of snow (the last aged in the freezer) for about a week.

The only relief from the routine of daily tests was provided by occasional survey flights, but I had ceased to look forward to them. With the birches in full leaf, our radioed wolves were mere hypothetical entities required to explain the movements of radio signals, like neutrinos or quarks, leaving tracks that could be glimpsed only rarely and with great effort.

To make matters worse, on one of my first flights I found all four members of the Upsala Lake pack miles from the den, which would never have been left unguarded if Freya had whelped. The absence of a litter was a disappointment, but at least I was able to see her, however briefly. The pack was weaving its way along an alder-choked logging road, and she lagged far enough behind the others that I was able to identify her by the position of her signal. The lead wolf, the largest of the four, stopped, looked over his shoulder, and waited until she caught up. She touched his nose with hers. The pups bounded up and tried to touch her nose, too, but the leader snapped at them, and they leaped away. Ahead of them the road dissolved into a small swamp. A white-flanked late-molting moose stood knee-deep in the algae-surfaced water at the far edge of the swamp. Shreds of loose fur hung from its pied flanks. Its head was in the water as the wolves reached the edge of the swamp.

The lead wolf froze, then turned to face the pack. This time all the wolves touched noses, then disappeared in the trees. A few minutes later a wolf charged from the trees nearest the moose. His momentum carried him to within three bodylengths of the moose, but his charge died quickly in the water, which was nearly as deep as he was tall. The moose raised its head and stood its ground. Two more wolves dived into the water and floundered toward their prey. The moose waded slowly into deeper water. One of the wolves swam after it, but the other two retreated to the shore. The swimming wolf paddled a wide circle around the moose, which was ripping up underwater plants and chewing them without evident concern. When the wolf completed his circle, he, too, gave up and splashed after the others.

I called Hunt as soon as I got back to the lab to tell him that Freya had had no pups. He took the news in stride. He had suspected as much, for all four wolves had been seen away from the den before, but only briefly and never this far. Lost litters were not uncommon, he said, especially in famine. He inquired about my experiment, and when I told him I had the information I needed, he suggested I use the rest of the time I'd allotted to check my results with the wolves at the Leta Park Zoo in Northton. These wolves were about to be released into a new, large enclosure, and when I finished my check, I might be able to design an experiment that would take advantage of the move—a sort of transplant in captivity. In my spare time I could collect anal-sac samples and run them on the gas chromatograph at the V A Hospital. This device was hooked up to a mass spectograph, so I could determine the identity of some of the fractions I'd yet to pin down. I was welcome to stay at his home, he added, and in fact, I'd be doing him a favor. He and the family were going on vacation, and I could house-sit. This last was what salesmen call the grabber. I agreed to meet him the next day at the Leta Park Zoo.

I met Hunt in the zoo parking lot. Before showing me the wolves, he unfurled on the hood of his car a map of a new zoo that would be built south of the new airport. "It'll make you feel a little better about this one." He pointed to a large area in the center of the map. "This is the wolf enclosure. We're trying for three acres, but it'll probably be smaller. This will be the showpiece," he continued, indicating two adjacent areas each twice the size of that allocated to the wolves. "The lions will be near the giraffes and zebras and other African ungulates, but you won't be able to see the fence that separates predators from prey." Hunt then pointed to a tiny corral behind us, where two emaciated wildebeests trudged in tedious circles in a cloud of flies. "Can't you just see those gnus running across the veldt?" he asked boyishly.

"All the gnus that's fit to sprint," I replied. Hunt winced and moved on.

We rounded the corner of the main building to find two wolves in a fairly large cage. "The white one is the alpha female, the gray one, her mate. The pups must be inside. Incidentally, the white one is the mother of Hurricane, the wolf Charlotte and I raised."

Here at last was a chance to find out about Hurricane. "You mention Hurricane in your book, but you don't explain what became of her. Where is she now?"

Hunt watched the white wolf in silence. Had I presumed on our professional relationship by bringing up a matter that was highly personal? Hunt drew a deep breath and began to speak in low, level tones. At first Hurricane had been as easy to keep as any puppy, but as she approached the end of her first year, she began to escape from the yard to run with neighborhood dogs. Upon her return from one midnight excursion Hunt had been forced to put her on a chain. She whined, paced, and leaped so desperately that Hunt could not bear the burden of her misery. The next day he drove her to the parking lot where Hunt and I had looked at the map. He left her in the car and called the zoo director, asking him to take Hurricane from the car and to care for her until he could find another zoo that would take her. He asked that the director never inform him where she went. "If I knew where she was," he concluded, "I'd want to see her, and seeing her in a cage would be more than I could stand."

We watched the caged wolves silently for another few seconds. Then Hunt led the way to the director's office.

We spent the afternoon installing apparatus for my experiments on Hurricane's mother and her pack. The evening was a confusion of packing and other preparations for the Hunts' departure in the morning. Miraculously Hunt had the whole clan in the station wagon by eight without threats or other coercion. In vain I tried to imagine what a vacation with Dr. Hunt would be like. Somehow I could not imagine his rising late to a day of fishing or golf. I fully expected him to return with a briefcase full of manuscripts, the curse and blessing of a life in which work and play are one.

The experiment at the zoo went smoothly, an unwelcome reminder of the advantages of work with subjects that are always where one wants them. The chromatography also went well, and by the time the Hunt family returned, I was ready to return to Ann Arbor.

13

Wolves Die

Lotte was free. At first she had flinched every twenty paces, as though bracing for an invisible fence, but soon she ran. For half the moonlit night she chased silvery shadows and windblown leaves. She tested her speed in an open forest, forelegs stretching parallel to the ground, then whipping beneath her again and again. Every few strides she was caught in a slanting moonbeam. In the darkness between them her black fur was lost in shadow; she seemed to flicker in and out of existence.

On one of her headlong runs she charged into a shallow stream. She scrambled onto the opposite bank, lay on the moss, and drank noisily. She dozed until dawn, when she was awakened by the sun in her eyes. She sneezed, rose, and stretched.

She loped along until she jumped a red squirrel that bounced easily to a tree and clung to its trunk just out of reach, chattering shrilly. A little farther on a hare, its coat prematurely patched with white, huddled in its form. She pounced on it and lay in a patch of sunlight to devour it.

She was thirsty again, so she trotted through the forest, testing the air.

A cool breeze carried a hint of moisture. She turned into the scent and soon saw a sun-spangled lake glittering through the trees. She froze in her tracks, then padded slowly to the rocky shore. She lapped the water in short bursts, raising her head every few seconds to glance around.

She turned right, but a fallen tree blocked her way. She whined, turned, and headed the other way, moving away from the shore to avoid boulders and blowdowns that were thicker there. After an hour of erratic progress she stopped to sniff and listen. A gust of wind rattled the few dry leaves still on the birches. She turned onto a trail that led toward the lake.

The trail opened onto a rocky beach. Two humans hunkered on the shore, ripping with blades at long silvery shapes, then dunking each one in the water. She trotted towards the men, running her bright red tongue over the long white teeth and her black muzzle. Her bushy tail wagged from side to side.

One of the fishermen heard something behind him. He glanced over his shoulder. "Jesus Christ," he whispered. His partner turned and froze, gaping in dread as the first fisherman reached for his tackle box. He withdrew a small revolver and started shooting even before he aimed.

The first shot missed. Lotte grabbed a fish then ran. The second shot missed, too, and she was halfway to the woods when the third hit her in the jaw. The small bullet did little damage but made her drop the fish. The fourth bullet glanced off a rib and tumbled through her lungs. She staggered, giving the fisherman time to aim the fifth and sixth shots, which lodged in her shoulders. She dropped behind a log, gasping.

205

The men were arguing as the one with the gun reloaded. He wanted to go after the wolf to finish it off. The other said he would be crazy to go into the woods after a wounded wolf.

Lotte heard the man approaching and raised her head. Blood ran from her open mouth. Her tail thumped weakly on the leaf-strewn ground. The man fired again. Lotte's neck arched slowly back until her muzzle pointed at the sky, then dropped limply onto the dead leaves.

The fishermen lashed her limp body to the hood of their jeep. All that evening they dragged it up and down the main street of Axe, until nothing was left but a dust and blood-caked swatch of black fur. They stopped at every bar but could not pay for their drinks. They were men of the hour; they had killed a wolf.

Hunt called me at my office to give me the news. Someone had failed to lock the wolf-pen gate; Lotte had pushed it open and strolled away. Red and Gray, who had tunneled out years before, had learned that freedom was not for them. They had remained at the open gate, whining, until Joe came out to see what was wrong.

My memory serves me well; it has erased the words with which I replied, leaving only an impression of their banality. I found myself standing at the window, looking across the quadrangle. I groped for a chair; my vision was misty. Some hint of emotion must have eluded my attempt to be matter-of-fact, for Hunt's next words were a condolence. He then began what was clearly an ill-disguised attempt to cheer me up and simultaneously to brace me for further ill tidings. Not Freya, I thought. Please don't let it be Freya.

It wasn't Freya, but it was almost as bad. Female One,

the last of the wandering transplants, had been shot. It was ironic that she, the smallest and shyest of the pack, and the first released, should be the last to go. She had never joined the others, and that had kept her alive, for she alone had remained in the wilderness near the release site. All the others had been killed as they wandered into more populated areas during the summer and early fall. The alpha male had died first, in July. He had been hit by a car on a straight stretch of highway. The other male had been killed later that month, shot in the head and chest with a small-caliber weapon.

The females had fared only slightly better. One had been trapped and shot in September, and Female One had made it until the week before, when she was shot by a deer hunter. A bullet had silenced her radio, but not before Moore traced her to the woods near a hunting shack. One of her ears had been removed, presumably as evidence for the bounty offered by the Wolf Hunters' Association. Hunt again offered his sympathy and said he'd see me in December.

A few weeks later my drive through the Thule Mountains was haunted by memories of dead wolves. Five of the ones I knew best had been killed by humans. A sixth, Muff, the transplant we'd released on Jack Pine Trail, had died soon thereafter, so humans, myself included, were implicated in her death, too. The herds of starving deer that lined the highways of the Thule Mountains were no distraction. A pall of death darkened my mood all the way to Ontolagon, and it was with more than my usual curiosity that I checked the flight sheets when I arrived. To my relief, Freya had been seen the previous day. She was with her pack, feeding on a kill a mile or so down the river.

Later that week I skied along the Ontolagon River, inspecting a series of kills made by Freya's pack. Some of them were only three-quarters eaten, meaning that the wolves might be back to finish them at any time. I knew I was in no danger, though. When Loki and Odin were pups, they might have been foolish enough to defend a kill against a human, but by now they were old enough to know better.

I skied in a large circle. The tracks suggested that only two wolves had walked up the river—one along the shore, the other well out on the ice. The deer and two other wolves had run from the woods. The deer had been intercepted by the wolves on the river. Evidence of strategic foresight? Perhaps, but the tracks didn't show when these events had taken place. The pair of wolves that had come from the shore might have run out long after the ones on the river had killed the deer.

Four sets of tracks leaving the kill led me to another, which had a little more meat on it than the first. These tracks showed the same pattern as the others. The Upsala Lake pack was either very lucky or had developed a superb system for killing deer.

My circle complete, I headed for the next kill. The shores receded as the river opened into Beach Lake. The sun was high, leaving me shadowless on a dazzling white plain. The distant horizon was a thin dark line of trees, the only division between the blinding snow and the light-filled air. I squinted against the glare and veered toward the dark spruce trees on the eastern shore. The forest shadows were a welcome relief. I kept close to them until the trees ended at a rocky point. Even before I rounded the point, a light breeze brought me the odor of the next kill.

The kill was closer than I thought—only 100 yards away

208

when it came into view. There was more of it left than I expected, too. It looked like most of it was still there. Then it moved. It was not a kill I had seen, but two wolves lying next to it. Upwind and busy, they had not yet detected me. I froze for a moment and then dropped slowly to my knees as I removed my pack to get my camera, never taking my eyes from the wolves. One of them rose and frisked around the other, which remained crouched, tearing at the deer. The frisky one nipped playfully at the other's tail. This brought a response: the other wolf rose, her dark mane and rufous coat identifying her as Freya. She pushed the other wolf away with a foreleg and returned to her meal. The push was gentle, but the playful one fell onto his side and rolled onto his back. He wagged his tail and waved his head from side to side until Freya licked his face.

I watched all this through my telephoto lens, afraid to snap the shutter for fear of alarming the wolves. Suddenly something startled them, and they made for the shore.

When I flew over the next morning, the deer was gone. Freya had either consumed it or carried it off to the shore, where it could be eaten without interference. I found the pack nearby, still hunting the eastern shore of Beach Lake. As I had surmised, the hunt did involve coordinated efforts by all four wolves. The yearlings ran through the woods on an erratic course but never went far from the shore. Frey patrolled the shore while Freya played free safety, keeping well out on the ice to intercept any deer jumped by the yearlings that might make it past her mate.

In this deadly game, each wolf's role was adapted to its abilities. The yearlings, who lacked the endurance needed for pursuit, were certainly capable of making a racket as they chased squirrels, hares, and each other through the brush. Freya, who had not completely recovered from the famine of the previous year, probably preferred to stay out on the windswept ice, where walking was easiest. Frey was an experienced hunter and strong enough to make his way through the deep snow that lay along the shore. He had certainly learned by now that the shore was a good place to hunt, with or without beaters and a backup. What all this meant was that there was no need to invoke planning or foresight to understand the behavior of the wolves. Once they had adopted their formation, for whatever reason, its effectiveness would soon become evident. As I knew only too well, plans can work without anyone's being aware of them.

It was not until that evening I realized these musings were, in their own way, almost as remarkable as the behaviors that inspired them, for though they were critical in tone, the inner voice that spoke them was not Hunt's but my own.

Whether insightful or blind, the pack's success along the Beach Lake shore did more than stave off starvation. Loki, now nearly two years old, returned to the remains of old kills while the rest of the pack continued south along the shore. When nothing, not even a skull or pelvis, was left, he struck off on his own, still traveling within the territory but no longer confined to the pack's usual routes, showing by his many shortcuts that he knew the territory well. I hoped that this independence was not a sign that he would leave the pack, for if the Upsala Lake wolves were to survive the deer decline, they would have to kill some moose, and killing a moose would require every wolf they had.

In fact, they would probably need more, or so I thought, until the Upsala Lake pack again displayed its uncanny ability to falsify any prediction as soon as it was made.

The wolves, joined once again by Loki, were picking their way through the rough and heavily wooded terrain in the center of their territory when they jumped a large bull moose from its bed. Ordinarily he would have stood his ground, but perhaps because he had been startled from sleep, he ran. His flight took him across Route 3 and into a fallen power line. The line had been abandoned years before, and the poles had collapsed, but the wire was still as strong as ever. It hung at antler height. The moose hit it running at top speed and dragged it for several yards before it brought him to a panting halt.

The wolves were close behind. The moose whirled clockwise to face them, winding a loop of wire around the base of one of his antlers. The wire terrified him even more than the wolves. He had dealt with wolves before, but never anything like this humming irresistible restraint. In panic he whirled again, clockwise. That instant would serve as well as any other to mark the moment of his death.

The wolves closed in. As they circled, they stayed just out of range of the moose's huge hooves. The moose circled, too, entangling himself further. In desperation he bolted, but there was just enough give to allow one step before the wire rebounded, knocking him to his knees. Instantly Freya was at his flank, slashing just behind his shoulder and jumping back before he could rise to kick. His breath flumed in the cold air. Blood welled in the wound. Now all the wolves had to do was wait.

Wolves are not always patient, especially not when they have drawn blood. Throughout the night they took turns snaking up to the moose to harry him with nips to nose and flank. Sometimes they worked singly and sometimes in pairs, but at least two wolves always rested for the next attack. By dawn the slash on the moose's flank had clotted, but he could barely stand.

His hooves, though still deadly, were becoming easier to dodge. Still, it was not until the sun was high that he suffered a mortal wound. Loki grabbed him high on the neck. The moose shook his head until Loki was hurled away, but it was the neck, not the jaws that gave. Maddened by the smell of blood, all the wolves attacked at once. Five minutes later the last of them fell gasping to the bloody snow. The moose still stood.

All the wolves but Loki lay still, recovering from their assault. Loki sat up, panting happily, watching the moose die. It was late afternoon when the moose fell to his knees. He bellowed again and again, each bellow rising in pitch at the end, each weaker than the one before. All the wolves got to their feet. Freya and her mate charged, knocking the moose onto his right side. They tore open the thick skin on his lower belly. The moose's legs went stiff, then relaxed.

The pack remained near the carcass for almost a week and returned at lengthening intervals for another ten days. The wolves' proximity to Route 3 provided Bert with two weeks of easy howling, but their sedentary habits during this period meant that I had to go far afield to find other packs to follow. It was a relief when they moved off for good. Bert and I walked in to inspect the remains of the moose. The head was still intact; still held erect by the wire, it was visible over the brush from thirty feet away. Until we were upon it, it was impossible to believe that the rest of it had been eaten. Half a dozen chickadees fluttered off the carcass to nearby branches.

I was waiting under the wing when Sam arrived at the plane at eight the next morning. I put the earphones on as soon as we were airborne and pointed south toward

Upsala Lake. I picked up Freya's signal as soon as we got some altitude. She and the rest of her pack were asleep on October Lake, at the bottom of a steep ridge.

I then switched to the frequency of a newly trapped wolf to the east. Instead of the faint beeps I expected, there was only an empty hiss. I signaled for more altitude but still got nothing. We spent the morning in a search pattern centered on Poobah Landing. When the pattern had expanded to cover an area five times the size of the wolf's range, I knew it was hopeless.

I called Hunt from the Transbush Airways office and gave him the news. He concluded our conversation with words strangely out of character for a dispassionate scientist who referred to wolves not by names but by numbers. "Probably the radio went out, but wolves do die," he said. "At least it wasn't Freya."

Our concern for Freya was soon revived when she and her pack went almost two weeks without a kill. Perhaps the deer along the Beach Lake shore had gotten wise to the pack's tricks, or perhaps there were simply too few left for the pack to have any chance of finding them. Freya and Frey began to hunt alone, leaving their offspring to gnaw at the head and bones of the moose.

Loki was unwilling to lie idle, however, and every few days he would strike out on his own, hunting for rabbits and beavers. His hunts, like those of his parents, were rarely successful.

As the end of breeding season drew near, our concern was not whether Freya would mate but whether she would survive.

14

Dispersal

Wolves have elaborate rituals for greeting but none at all for farewell. Freya's pack was no exception. Whenever Loki returned from one of his solitary hunts, he was welcomed by boisterous barks and leaps, but his departures were seldom noted. Late one morning Freya led her pack north to hunt along the Ontolagon River; Loki simply went south, going his own way without a backward glance, as he had so many times before. He soon reached Jack Pine Trail, which marked the territory's southern border. This time he did not turn back but crossed the road without hesitation. He had become a lone wolf.

A week later Loki was still wandering. He had yet to kill a deer, but he had caught several hares and a beaver. One sunny afternoon he crouched atop a sunny bank, watching a hole in the ice that sealed a beaver pond. Eventually the beaver would have to come out to feed. Loki did not mind waiting, for time to him was only the interval between events, and there was plenty going on. Small shifts in the cool breeze coming from the pond brought him news of the distant woods: thawing of rotten wood; a rattle of tiny claws on rough bark; cries of birds. The sun's warmth invited a nap, but the wolf's yellow eyes never left the pond.

The black water shifted, rising and falling in the hole as though it were breathing. A triangular nose and two beady eyes broke the surface. The nose twitched, and the eyes darted back and forth, but the wind was in the wolf's favor. The beaver failed to notice that among the blurred forms on the bank above there was one without a mantle of snow.

The huge rodent heaved itself onto the ice and paddled forward, half crawling, half swimming through the slushy snow. When his quarry was a body length away from the hole, Loki plunged down the bank. The beaver's eyes were as sensitive to motion as they were oblivious to form, and at the wolf's first movement the ungainly creature whirled and scrambled back to safety with astonishing speed. The wolf arrived just in time to catch the geyser of spray splashed by the beaver's flat tail.

From the safety of the pond the beaver watched Loki shake himself dry. Then, rolling insouciantly onto its back, the rodent swam around the edge of the open water, just out of reach. Loki ran alongside, barking and whimpering. After three complete circuits the enraged wolf poised himself to leap. The beaver rolled quickly onto its belly, drenched the wolf with another smack of its tail, and was gone. Loki shook himself again and climbed slowly back up the bank to dry and wait. He had had nothing to eat, but neither had the beaver. Sooner or later it would emerge again.

The next day Loki had moved off to the southwest, but a bloody patch of snow thirty feet from the hole in the ice showed that he had waited long enough.

Over the next couple of weeks Loki moved steadily southwest until he was only twenty miles from the suburbs of Baraga. The young wolf had learned enough of the ways of people to veer north as soon as he encountered signs of a human habitation. Eventually he settled down at the edge of the national forest, found a mate, and founded a pack of his own. The cycle was complete; Freya had raised him well.

His mother's life was little changed by his departure. The brutal business of survival left no time for any regret Freya might have felt at the loss of her son. The few deer that remained in the territory could be taken by three wolves about as well as by four, and each wolf's share was now a little larger. The emigration of Loki had not hampered the pack's ability to hunt moose. There had always been too few for that; the one they had chased into the power line had been a fluke.

Such were my thoughts one cold March morning as I skied along the Upsala Lake pack's trail. Plausible as these considerations were, however, I was soon led to wonder whether or not I might once again have underestimated the wolves I knew best. Somewhere ahead a chain saw alternately sang and muttered. The racket suggested rage subsiding into irritation at the dumb indifference of trees. How, I wondered, would the wolves react to this intrusion?

The answer came immediately, in the form of three sets of tracks turning abruptly left, leaving the trail for the brush. Evidently the wolves had been even less anxious to venture near the new clear-cut than I was. After detouring around the clearing, the wolves had swung gradually right until they intercepted the continuation of the abandoned logging road they had been following. After another half mile they had once again turned left to enter the woods. This time, however, they had fanned out, running through deep snow that slowed them to a walk. Even so, each wolf had continued to plow a separate furrow. Three parallel trenches moved through an open gallery forest of spruce and birch. The left and middle trails converged on a small trampled bowl. I could imagine the nose touching and tail wagging of the wolves that made it. The rest of the tracks were not so easy to interpret, but an hour later I had pieced together a pretty good idea of what had happened.

The two wolves who touched noses had continued on their way, now running single file. A bull moose, browsing in a small swale just ahead, left a pile of pellets and ran. The wolves charged from the left, so the moose ran obliquely to the right, toward the third wolf, which came in on his flank, herding him away from the road. The pack fell into a single file behind the moose. Even though he was breaking trail for the wolves, he drew steadily away from them. His long legs, used to the resistance of water, whipped through the heavy snow as though it were fog. A bounding gait would carry him faster and create rougher going for the wolves, but bounding was not necessary. He could hear the wolves falling farther and farther behind.

Suddenly empty space gaped before him. He dodged to the right, but the slanting trunk of a fallen tree blocked his way. He whirled to find the wolves close behind him, already abreast, heads lowered, moving in one step at a time. With a stateliness that matched the tempo of the advance, he lowered his antlers until the sharp tines that

217

rimmed the fan-shaped plates were directed at the largest of the wolves. This wolf sprang, leaping steeply, as though trying to jump over the antlers. The moose tossed his head, but the spring was a feint—the wolf clamped his jaws on the moose's pendulous nose. The wolf somehow held on as he was whipped from side to side by violent jerks of the massive head. Meanwhile, the others sprang at belly and haunch.

A flick of a long foreleg sent the first wolf flying. A quick step backward put the moose in position to stomp the second, but as he raised a hind leg, the wolf rolled away. A kick with the same leg connected solidly with the third wolf, and lifted the wolf out of the snow. It fell back and skulked away, whimpering.

The moose tenderly explored his injured nose with his long tongue as the wolves regrouped. Again they moved in slowly side by side. Just as they came into range of hooves and antlers, they sprang in unison. For an instant all three wolves were in the air. Then they hit, one on the neck, the others high on back and haunch. The moose withstood the impact easily but shifted a foreleg for a wider stance. The hoof hit ice-covered rock and slipped. The moose tried to recover, but it was too late: his weight was committed to a hoof that slid off the edge of the cliff. What had looked like firm footing was an overhanging cornice of frozen snow. The moose rolled onto his right side as he fell.

The wolves rode the moose down in a shower of snow. Their fall was broken by his body when it thudded onto bare rock beneath the overhanging cornice. Before the huge animal could expand his cracked ribs for another breath, the wolves were at his throat and belly. He had no chance to rise. He kicked furiously, and then, except

*for the vapor steaming from strewn entrails and the oc-
casional spasm of unsurrendered muscle, he lay still.*

The Upsala Lake pack ate well that week. There was
still meat on the ribs and marrow in the bones when the
wolves left the kill. They returned at irregular and lengthening intervals until all that remained were a rug of hair,
a few scattered fragments of bone, and a pair of antlers.

The flanking maneuver at the beginning of the hunt
suggested an attempt to drive the moose toward the cliff,
but I would never know whether it was planning or ac-
cident that led to the kill. In any case, the kill was a good
omen, for whether by foresight or blind luck, if the Upsala
Lake wolves could chase one moose into a power line and
another over a cliff, they might be able to kill more and
not have to depend on the ever-diminishing supply of deer.

Though the kill boded well for Freya, it was a bad sign
for me. The incident illustrated the vanity of inferences
about the intelligence of wolves by observing their behavior of tracks. Driving a moose over a cliff was the best
demonstration of strategic thinking I could hope to find,
but even this episode could plausibly be ascribed to chance.
I was near the end of my last winter on the wolf project,
and it was time to take a hard look at what I'd learned.

A table of shortcuts and detours taken by the wolves
I'd tracked supported my claim that wolves used mental
maps, but I had not eliminated all the alternatives. I let
my eyes wander along the bookshelf over my desk. I did
a tiny double take as my gaze swept past the red notebook
that contained the maps drawn by the people we'd taken
on walks through the woods three summers before. Driven
more by my desire to escape the baleful blankness of my
unstarted dissertation than by any hope of inspiration, I

pulled the notebook down and leafed through the maps. Again I was amazed at how different they were: some neatly drafted; others hastily scrawled. It was hard to believe that they represented the same area and that they did so with the same features. Yet there they were: edges, routes, regions, and landmarks, each neatly circled and labeled. I then pulled out my field notes and opened the notebook to my first sketch, a map of the rendezvous site where Hunt and I had watched the pups at play. I had drawn the location of all the scats I'd seen there; the whole area was covered with the little d's I used to represent them. Next was my first winter sample of tracks, left by Freya. As usual, she had marked her route well; her scent marks formed a chain across the northern edge of her territory.

I leafed ahead to my second winter, when Freya had taken the same route. This time she had been traveling in the opposite direction but had marked the same landmarks as she had the previous winter.

I realized for the first time that my sketches were almost as diverse as those of our human subjects. Some showed beeline routes from one deer yard to another; others, the tangled skein of tracks wolves left as they hunted their way through one of these regions. Then there were the scent marks on the scalloped series of approaches and withdrawals along the shore of Border Lake, left by a pack tracing the northern edge of its territory. Too bad I couldn't train a wolf to draw its own map.

Then it hit me. Perhaps the wolves *had* drawn maps. Their patterns of scent marking were complex but certainly not random. They did not simply mark whatever happened to be there; they selected certain features, the very features that humans draw to make a map: not merely landmarks (like rocks or tufts of grass at the beginning of a shortcut or detour), but also routes, regions (like the area around a rendezvous site), and edges (the rate of scent marking doubles when a pack reaches a territorial border). In short, wolves mark what people draw.

These parallels could be coincidental, but these features are what one must remember to find one's way, whether one is a human or a wolf. In my dissertation I argued that the shortcuts, detours, and multiple approach routes used by wolves show that they have mental maps and that their patterns of scent marking suggest that the elements of these maps are similar to those of humans. I did, however, resist the temptation to title my dissertation "The Naked Wolf."

Evidently my committee found my arguments convincing, or perhaps they simply wished to forestall my offer to read at length from my field notes during my defense. In any case, with their blessing I received my degree.

With the ordeals of writing, revising, and defense behind me, I paid a last visit to the wolf project. Axe was much the same as on my first visit. The airport now handled jets, and the tourists were more numerous, but the forest was as close as ever. Hunt had expanded his operations and had radios on twenty-three wolves, two lynx, a marten, and a fisher. The deer population had reversed its decline, and there were signs that the number of wolves in the forest had found a new equilibrium. The Olympus pack's territory had been divided up among neighboring packs. Freya's mate, Frey, had disappeared, but she had a new one. On the last day of my visit I made a pilgrimage to the burn where it all began. The waterfall was still there, the boulders were still bright pink, but the jack pine seedlings were now knee-high. On the slope where Hunt and I had watched the pups I found a few fresh scats. I brought one home.

Epilogue

"Thomas Hunt" and "Bert Cartwright" are still doing wolf research, sometimes together. I am in the Four Corners Area, learning to write.

Shortly after I left the wolf project Red and Gray escaped from their pen and were immediately shot by a vigilant neighbor. An open-pit mine larger than the one at "Gantry" is planned for Freya's territory, but as I write these words, she and her mate (her fourth) are still marking the trails south of the Ontolagon.